**W9-ABR-497**

*Wendy Wasserstein*

# Wendy Wasserstein

## Dramatizing Women, Their Choices and Their Boundaries

*by*

GAIL CIOCIOLA

McFarland & Company, Inc., Publishers
*Jefferson, North Carolina and London*

CARL A. RUDISILL LIBRARY
LENOIR-RHYNE COLLEGE

Except where noted, all excerpts from *Uncommon Women and Others, Isn't It Romantic,* and *The Heidi Chronicles* (©1990, 1985, 1984, 1978 by Wendy Wasserstein) appear in *The Heidi Chronicles and Other Plays* published by Harcourt Brace Jovanovich in 1990.

All excerpts from *The Sisters Rosensweig* (© 1993 by Wendy Wasserstein) appear in *The Sisters Rosensweig* published by Harcourt Brace in 1993.

All excerpts from *An American Daughter* appear in the February Draft of the rehearsal script (1997) or, as cited, in the First Draft (1995) of Wendy Wasserstein's unpublished manuscripts of the play.

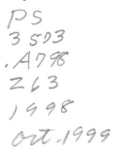

British Library Cataloguing-in-Publication data are available

Library of Congress Cataloguing-in-Publication Data

Ciociola, Gail, 1948–
    Wendy Wasserstein : dramatizing women, their choices and their
boundaries / by Gail Ciociola.
        p.   cm.
    Includes bibliographical references and index.
    ISBN 0-7864-0523-6 (library binding : 50# alkaline paper) ∞
    1. Wasserstein, Wendy—Characters—Women.  2. Women and
literature—United States—History—20th century.  I. Title
PS3573.A798Z63   1998
812'.54—dc21                                         98-12339
                                                       CIP

©1998 Gail Ciociola. All rights reserved

*No part of this book may be reproduced or transmitted in any form or by any means, electronic or mechanical, including photocopying or recording, or by any information storage and retrieval system, without permission in writing from the publisher.*

Manufactured in the United States of America

*McFarland & Company, Inc., Publishers*
    *Box 611, Jefferson, North Carolina 28640*

LENOIR-RHYNE COLLEGE

# Acknowledgments

Several people assisted me throughout the writing of this work and deserve special mention. First and foremost, I must thank Betsy Fifer who, during this book's life as a dissertation, became much more to me than just a thesis director. As my mentor and comforter, she understood the complexities of juggling this project with my full and part time jobs and made it possible for us to work via her home, her phone, and her mailbox.

I also wish to thank Jim Frakes and Rosemarie Arbur for their input; they served not only on my dissertation committee but also on my examination committee. I also appreciate the willingness of Pam Pepper, who, without knowing much about me, agreed to participate in my dissertation as the outside-of-department contributor.

One thing that stands out above all from doing this study is that many, many people truly adore and respect Wendy Wasserstein. Everyone I contacted during my research seemed to leap at the mention of her name and provide me with—in some cases—immediate assistance. In this vein, I thank Kim Powers of WNET in New York for lending me a cassette of the PBS presentation of *Uncommon Women and Others*; Erin Sanders of Second Stage for mailing me that play's revival script; Lucy LePage of Royce Carlton Agency for directing my earliest inquiries to the right places; the editors of *New Women* for returning my call late one night and looking up page numbers I needed for my bibliography; and Patricia Albright of the Mount Holyoke College Archives for retrieving the mounds of Wasserstein material for me.

Of all these "strangers" who willingly assisted my efforts, however, I must especially thank Jenny Lyn Bader, Wendy Wasserstein's personal assistant. Jenny returned all my calls, mailed me notes, sent me the telescript for *Antonia and Jane*, and—incredibly—also sent me with the blessing and extraordinary generosity of the playwright herself, two drafts for *An American Daughter*, one of them long before it went into even workshop production. Jenny Lyn also arranged that very important interview I had with Wendy and phoned me near midnight the day before to assure me that my luncheon with Wendy was really happening.

On a personal note, I thank Pat Wertman for providing me with meals during the long and uninterrupted hours of writing; Michael Ripchinski, a former student of mine, for his invaluable contributions as research assistant and taskman; and two people, who, little known to them, began my writing career some forty years ago: my mother, who wrote my first sentences with me, and my father, who told me that English was my most important subject.

Finally, I thank you, Wendy. For writing these wonderful plays, for spending well over two hours with me on a hot August Saturday in Picholine's Restaurant in New York City, and for calling me with good wishes and project updates before I sent this manuscript to my publisher.

You are most definitely an uncommon woman.

# Contents

*Acknowledgments*     v

1. Wendy Wasserstein: Feminism, Feminist
   Drama, and Fem-en(act)ment     1

2. Wasserstein's Uncommon Women     21

3. Having It All: A Woman Is (Not) Her Mother     40

4. "All in This Together": Idealism, Sisterhood,
   and Other Dilemmas     56

5. Of Life and Men     81

6. What Price Glory?     100

7. Fem-en(act)ment Revisited     127

*Appendix: New York City and Television Production
History of the Major Plays of Wendy Wasserstein*     139

*Bibliography of Works by Wasserstein*     143

*Bibliography of Critical Works and Reviews*     149

*Bibliography of General Works*     157

*Index*     165

# 1

# Wendy Wasserstein: Feminism, Feminist Drama, and Fem-en(act)ment

## Fem-en(act)ment: Toward a Definition

Although Wendy Wasserstein originally envisioned *The Heidi Chronicles* as a "history of the Women's Movement" (Betsko 431), her Pulitzer Prize–winning play recounts the personal chronicle of one woman, as the title suggests, more than it tells the political one of all women. Depicting the impact of the late twentieth century women's movement on the fictitious Heidi Holland, Wasserstein examines how Heidi struggles between her college years and midlife with what T. E. Kalem describes in *Uncommon Women and Others* as "the expanding, unnerving world of women's goals and options" (111). In light of Wasserstein's previous and subsequent major plays, however, it seems clear that the impact of the feminist movement on those whom she names "uncommon women and others" has generated a stylistic and thematic impulse not only in *The Heidi Chronicles* but in these other dramas as well. In the present book, therefore, I examine Wendy Wasserstein's major plays as an œuvre devoted to sociopolitical and literary objectives that I call "fem-en(act)ment" and establish that Wasserstein utilizes fem-en(act)ment primarily as a cyclic rendering of the impact of the women's movement on private life.

"Fem-en(act)ment" as word and concept provides a functional means by which Wasserstein's plays can be best understood as philosophy and as literary genre and style. It reflects what Mary Daly

1

calls gynomorphic language, a reworking of linguistic systems to create new words and produce meanings vital to women's ends (*Gyn/Ecology* xi). Constructed as such, its fragmented components yield the principal contexts: "fem," for female perspective *and* feminist intent; "(act)," for stage drama; and "en(act)ment," for the revelation and successful execution of one's overall motifs and motives. As a whole, then, fem-en(act)ment is textual or performance drama that, guided by a feminist disposition, thematically *and* stylistically enacts situations of interest to women, the psychological and social effects of which form the core of that drama.

It is important to note that in itself fem-en(act)ment does not advance a specific feminist agenda. The current climate of feminist debate, however, makes it difficult to acknowledge whether one's position is indeed feminist and by extension whether a playwright's work is indeed feminist. For this reason, I would like to clarify my vision of feminism and feminist drama and, most importantly, to locate Wasserstein's position in both.

## WASSERSTEIN'S FEMINISM: AN OVERVIEW

Although she refers to herself as a humanist, Wasserstein wields a good bit of political rhetoric, often under the cloak of humor, by framing her approaches from a viewpoint that she herself could not imagine to be anything but feminist. In a series of articles for *Harper's Bazaar* called "The Wendy Chronicles," for instance, she has comically attacked the lack of female character actors in Hollywood, lamented "lesbian chic" as a fashion statement divorced of any real human-rights stance, and downplayed the significance of the electoral Year of the Woman (1992) by noting that "365 days was all we were given" ("Backlash Blues" 77). As these examples indicate, Wasserstein not only calls attention to certain ethical situations significant to women but also advocates a position that she, as well as a public prone to generalizations, would define as feminist.

Contrary to public perception, however, there is no such thing as feminism. It exists, instead, as a categorization of study and practice just as diverse in scope, for instance, as psychology. As Lynda

Hart notes, "feminism has become feminisms" (Hart and Phelan 7), a myriad of different and sometimes conflicting ideas about how women define themselves and their needs. Theoretical texts designed to label the sources and dimensions of various first- and second-wave movements, for instance, identify specific feminist approaches such as liberal, cultural, materialist, psychoanalytic, radical, and existential. Many third-wave feminists of the 1990s, on the other hand, appear to eschew these labels in favor of what Jill Dolan dismisses as "playful pluralism" (*Spectator* 3) or to distance themselves from them altogether. For this reason, a public or media declaration that Wasserstein's positions reflect feminist thinking—even though that estimation appears not only obvious but accurate—requires a different kind of exploration in the context of scholarly considerations.

While Dinah Leavitt maintains that the "specific way in which each ... performer defines 'feminist' is very important to an understanding of that ... individual's work" (9), Wasserstein seems to favor a pluralistic blend of feminism. She reveals signs of liberal, cultural, and materialist thinking, and as a whole seems to advance contemporary "power feminism" (Wolf, *Fire* 137). Of the first three types, Wasserstein's major plays predominantly espouse the liberal feminist ethic of equality between the sexes and, in particular, of achieving parity with men in the workplace and at home. In *The Heidi Chronicles*, for instance, this conviction underscores Heidi Holland's observation to Scoop Rosenbaum that all women deserve to "fulfill their potential" rather than spend a lifetime of "making you and your children tuna-fish sandwiches" (173).

According to its critics, liberal feminism relies on a value system claimed to be universal. On one hand, it ignores differences among women and assumes that they all strive for the same things, for instance, as Heidi Holland, an art historian with a Ph.D. Although the critics have a valid point that liberal feminism does not adequately recognize racial, class, and value differences among women, Wasserstein does not pretend to speak for all women. As Chapter 2 will demonstrate in more detail, her main characters are not every woman, but college-educated and career-driven "uncommon women" determined to "fulfill their potential" even when they have not reached certainty about the direction of that potential. More important to Wasserstein's liberal feminism than quibbling about the notion that not all women subscribe to the same values is that they probably do subscribe to achieving *whatever* they choose without fear of sexual discrimination or, perhaps, of pitting their job concerns against their private ones.

A second objection is that "the universally human" to which liberal feminists write is "still based on the male model" (Dolan, *Spectator* 3, 5), making some critics uneasy about calling the liberal faction feminist at all. While some of the values embraced by Wasserstein's "uncommon women," especially regarding their quest for power and parity in the marketplace, have evolved largely from male experience and standards, my problem with the critics lies in the essentialist tone that does not acknowledge that some of those values, regardless of their origin, might be worth valorizing even if others, like enforced gender roles, are not. The "universally human" to which the critics refer is, in fact, more familiarly known as Wasserstein's self-described platform of humanism, and although Toril Moi for one has voiced objections specifically to "humanism" (87), there is, it seems, room here as well as in feminism for the "playful pluralism" to which Dolan objects. It allows Wasserstein, for example, to abandon traditional models of femininity and gender roles, which humanism may or may not advance, and suggests that her humanism probably evolves from the underlying belief in an individual's dignity.

Wasserstein's predilection toward cultural feminism, or "difference feminism" (Young, "Perspective" M3), aligns less with its theoretical reification of sexual difference and female superiority than it does with the creative processes of form and style in which she writes her plays both individually and as an œuvre. This will be examined more closely in the context of feminist drama, but I should note that in literary practice, cultural feminism is frequently associated with the mother-daughter paradigm. Wasserstein's most obvious treatment of this appears in *Isn't It Romantic*; however, it also materializes to some extent in both *The Sisters Rosensweig* and *An American Daughter*, and to a lesser degree in *The Heidi Chronicles*.

As they do with liberal feminism, critics allege among other things that while cultural feminists favor so-called female values over those purportedly endorsed by men, they ignore the differences among women, as though there exists a "mythic subject Woman" replete with a feminized version of "transcendent, universal" identity (Dolan, *Spectator* 10, 9). According to Dolan, the emphasis on the mother-daughter motif, in particular, reflects a failure to deconstruct "family-structured gender policies" (*Spectator* 9), which not only alienate those women uncomfortable with the traditional family formula but also involve a dangerously close alliance with biological determinism.

Wasserstein has characterized *Isn't It Romantic* as a play about "single women and their mothers" (*Bachelor Girls* 30). I don't disagree with this estimation, but I think "a play about single women and their mothers and the way they all made their life choices" would more accurately reflect its content. In other words, as Chapter 3 will discuss, while situations in the play whirl about two daughters and their mothers, the relationships themselves do not form the thematic core of the play. Nonetheless, even if they did, it would seem ridiculous to accuse Wasserstein of automatically promulgating some family agenda, which in itself also does not necessarily constitute an antifeminist position.

More enlightening about Wasserstein's mother-daughter motif, perhaps, is what the œuvre's situations and themes reveal with regard to it. Contrary to traditional family structure, for one thing, the never-married Heidi Holland in *The Heidi Chronicles* adopts a child alone; Tess Goode lives on-and-off with her twice-divorced, currently unmarried mother, Sara, in *The Sisters Rosensweig*; and, in *An American Daughter*, Lyssa Dent Hughes professes barely to have known not only her mother, who died when she was 14, but also two of her three subsequent stepmothers. But let's establish the crucial point: Wasserstein's governing emphasis in these plays, as well as in *Uncommon Women and Others* and, in my opinion, *Isn't It Romantic*, lies not with mothers and daughters but with the independent nature of these "uncommon women" and the forces behind all their life choices. Despite the critics' reservations, understandable in light of dominant cultural ideology, mothers and daughters occupy a large space in the collective psyche, and Wasserstein's inclusions, subtle or otherwise, operate mainly as subtext not pretext.

Ultimately, as suggested, life choices dominate the scope of Wasserstein's drama. Believing that all women "deserve to fulfill their potential," Wasserstein consistently intertwines this idea with the elusive prospect of "having it all" or of having that successful balance of career and family that Betty Friedan termed the "feminist mystique" (*Second Stage* 27). As her plays painfully reveal and as subsequent chapters will demonstrate, neither Wasserstein nor her characters fully resolve the dilemmas posited by the feminist mystique, since both are apparently resigned to an "either/or" fissure of family versus career.

Wasserstein's scrutiny of this process and of the pressures and misgivings associated with it constitutes, in a limited sense, a materialist feminist approach. Materialist feminism, the currently preferred term to its predecessors, Marxist feminism and socialist feminism, is informed by the latters' most important common variable, the examination of the material conditions of women's lives. To some, all feminist movements do this, but in theory and in literary criticism, materialist feminism more pointedly attempts to "disrupt the narrative gender ideology, to denaturalize gender as representation, and to demystify the workings of the genderized representational apparatus itself" (Dolan, *Spectator* 101). For example, then, materialist feminism represents the idea that since power is "not inherently male, a woman who assumes a dominant role is only malelike if the culture considers power as a solely male attribute" (Dolan, *Spectator* 68).

The material condition on which Wasserstein focuses most consistently is that "uncommon women" do struggle with the previously noted "either/or" predicament as they pursue their life choices. Unlike a staunch materialist, however, she does not quite challenge the dominant cultural ideology that men can have both a career and family without the same inner turmoil that women experience in first seeking and then balancing the two. Instead of challenging the ideology, she mainly shows her characters' attempts—however unsuccessful—to adjust their lives around it. In the process, she doggedly maintains the same perspective throughout the œuvre, for even though she sometimes takes on the persona of a mere observer of feminist angst, she persistently maintains her belief that a woman is entitled to pursue both her professional goals and private desires without sacrificing one for the other and in particular without sacrificing the former for the latter.

Because this position manifests itself regardless of what form of second-wave feminism she evinces, Wasserstein essentially identifies with contemporary power feminism. Technically, this is little more than neoliberal feminism, especially since it promotes ideas of equality and self-empowerment but without the benefit of a clear theoretical impulse. Unfortunately, however, power feminism has also been unfairly parlayed into a binary opponent of what the media and some feminists have characterized as "victim feminism," dubiously defined by Naomi Wolf as "seek[ing] power through an identity of powerlessness" (*Fire* 135).

Though Wasserstein would certainly disavow victim feminism by Wolf's standard, she has acknowledged frequently that sexual discrimination has led to the underrepresentation of women in all aspects of theater production, a condition that to "victim feminists" indicates what battlegrounds they should address. Consequently, as further exploration will confirm, Wasserstein's locus in this heavily publicized debate—at times, an almost nasty one—is actually compatible with the underlying premises of each side.

Proponents of power feminism include, most notably, Wolf, Christina Hoff Sommers, Rene Denfeld, and Katie Roiphe, although even they do not always agree with one another. Denfeld probably speaks for all, however, when she complains that the "empowering vision has been turned on its head in feminism today" by "ideological extremism," such as antipornographer Catherine MacKinnon's, which "casts women as helpless babes" in a way that "dismisses our strength." In addition, says Denfeld, the "perception that being a feminist means hating men is a major reason why so many women who support equality don't want anything to do with the [women's] movement" ("Feminist Movement" A27).

Sommers, in particular, has attacked what she calls "gender feminists" who fuel this so-called war between the sexes. In *Who*

Wendy Wasserstein

*Stole Feminism? How Women Have Betrayed Women*, she suggests that "gender feminists" ignore the significant gains achieved by women and cites Susan Faludi's *Backlash* as an example, she says, of faulty research aimed at uncovering and condemning ongoing patriarchal compliance in female subjugation and victimization.

In "I'm Not a Feminist But I Play One on TV," Faludi dismisses this contingent as made up of "Pod Feminists" (32) whose "co-opted language of 'empowerment' and 'reconciliation'" with men (33) reduces them to "feminist denouncers" (34) who audaciously call themselves feminists to a media giddy to play "gotcha journalism" (38). Saying that outrage and vocalization against harassment, coercion, and pornography are in themselves exemplary of action and antithetical to victim politics, Faludi notes that "[f]eminism identifies victimization not so we can wallow in it, but so we can wallop it" (36).

"Anti-feminist feminists," claims Leora Tanenbaum, are a conservative element who "do acknowledge, to a small extent, the dangers of sexism and the power of sexist institutions, but they advocate individualistic coping mechanisms" (12). Both she and Faludi argue, in fact, that in the name of rugged individualism and self-empowerment, the "antifeminist feminists" betray a naive assessment of gender politics and have avoided the difficult arena of protest and serious political action needed for the guarantee of women's rights.

As stated already, Wasserstein evinces a particularly instructive position in this fray. For example, despite the materialist feminist investigation into the cultural constraints of power, Wasserstein herself never considers such constraints relevant exclusively to masculine behavior. Reflecting the central premise of power feminism, in fact, she constructs a rather extraordinary base of power in and about the business careers of Lillian Cornwall (*Isn't It Romantic*) and Sara Goode, and throughout the academic and medical worlds of, respectively, Heidi Holland and Lyssa Dent Hughes. If anything, Wasserstein assumes that the desire to define and achieve self-empowerment motivates all of her "uncommon women," and consequently she not only rejects any tendency to resigned victimization—or to hating men, for that matter—but also eschews the kind of "ideological extremism" to which Denfeld also objects.

On the other hand, Wasserstein recognizes, like Faludi and Tanenbaum, that sexual discrimination still exists and that power feminism, for this reason, still necessitates some activism and protective legislation. In *The Heidi Chronicles*, for instance, her main character displays an unmistakable sense of self-empowered awareness and initiative from the onset of the play by single-mindedly pursuing a career as an art historian. However, once Heidi becomes a committed feminist, she also becomes politically involved by marching in protest against the lack of museum retrospectives for women artists.

Furthermore, as noted earlier, Wasserstein herself manifests the kinds of activity that Faludi deems essential to women's rights by speaking out in her lectures and essays on behalf of numerous feminist positions. Her contribution to "Our Bodies No More," which appreciatively mentions both Marilyn French and the much-maligned Faludi, provides a particularly significant example of activism by implying the need for de jure protection of women's "control over their own bodies" (229).

By synthesizing the oppositions of this current and inflammatory state of feminist dialogue, Wasserstein by extension also expands herself further into the pluralistic mode she favors. As this synthesis and the entire overview demonstrate, then, a scholarly analysis of her location in theoretical and practical feminism confirms what a perhaps less-informed observer might already conclude: that in light of the diverse strains of liberal, cultural, and materialist feminism in her work, as well as a penchant for contemporary power feminism, Wendy Wasserstein cultivates a feminist disposition convincingly.

## WASSERSTEIN AND FEMINIST DRAMA: AN OVERVIEW

Although a feminist impulse pervades and sustains each play in Wasserstein's œuvre, this impulse does not in itself, however, automatically create "feminist drama." As a specific genre, "feminist drama" encompasses matters regarding style and message that require further discussion and clarification.

According to Gayle Austin, "not all plays by or about women need be stimulated by feminist theory" (*Feminist Theories* 93). Although a pluralistic mix does—consciously or unconsciously—inform Wasserstein's material, she began writing *Uncommon Women and Others* in 1973 at the Yale School of Drama mainly because the representation of women in her assigned readings of Jacobean drama appalled her. Men "were kissing the skulls of women and dropping dead from the poison," she says. "And I thought, this is not familiar to me" (Finn 360). Interestingly, because the play examines female life, a male student dismissed it as meaningless to him, thereby angering Wasserstein. "I thought, I spent my life getting into *Hamlet* and *Lawrence of Arabia*, so why don't you try it" (Finn 360).

Wasserstein's experience in this situation exemplifies her confrontation with what feminist film critic Laura Mulvey identifies as the "male gaze," a voyeuristic and narcissistic phenomenon in which cinema—and, by association, drama—represents women as erotic objects for male pleasure and depicts the hero as a figure with whom the male spectator identifies (16–19). As Wasserstein said years after the Yale incident, when women attend the theater, there "should be something for them" (Cohen 261).

Identifying what that "something" means and how it materializes in film, stage, or script as a feminist undertaking, however, comprises the ongoing debate among feminist performance critics. As Dinah Leavitt observes, little agreement exists about the nature of feminist drama except that it focuses on women's experiences (12). In fact, one of the reasons that I have coined the expression "fem-en(act)ment" to suit my own purposes is that research regarding women as authors and subjects of drama reveals a somewhat confusing array of terminology, such as "feminist drama," "feminist theater," and "woman-conscious" drama, each of which applies only somewhat satisfactorily to Wasserstein.

Rosemary Curb, for instance, prefers the phrase "woman-conscious" drama, which she defines as "all drama by and about women that is characterized by multiple interior reflections of women's lives and perceptions" (302). Since Wasserstein frequently evinces the mode of "multiple interior reflections," most notably in *Uncommon Women and Others* and *The Heidi Chronicles*, she does conform to

Curb's criteria. Circumscribed as such, "woman-conscious" drama seems laudably democratic, but it dangerously—though inadvertently, perhaps—leaves room for plays that could defend female subservience, domestic or otherwise, as bliss, a troubling proposition antithetical to Wasserstein's feminism.

According to the criteria by which critics understand the term, Wasserstein also does not write "feminist theater." Functioning specifically as "rhetorical enterprises [whose] primary aim is action, not art" (Patti Gillespie 286), feminist theater, best exemplified in the collaborative approaches of feminist theater groups such as the Split Britches company of New York and the Rhode Island Feminist Theater, exists primarily as a persuasive tool meant to bolster or influence feminist beliefs and political activity. These "inherently radical" productions, according to Elizabeth Natalle, frequently disrupt conventional representational apparatus and dominant gender ideology, such as compulsory heterosexuality, and "do not operate within the boundaries of commercial theater." Citing *The Heidi Chronicles* specifically, Natalle notes that Wasserstein belongs, unlike feminist theater writers, to an "independent set of women playwrights (often with a feminist vision) who write for more mainstream audiences" (115).

Wasserstein does, however, write feminist *drama*. "If the agent is a woman, her purpose autonomy, and the scene an unjust sociosexual hierarchy," says Janet Brown, "the play is a feminist drama" (16). Fulfilling Brown's description—which, in short, tailors character, theme, and plot to feminist intent—Wasserstein's major characters are women at odds with existing sociosexual traditions that make their desire to achieve autonomy and balance private desires with professional ones problematic. What separates this from "woman-conscious" drama is the emphasis on "autonomy"; what separates it from feminist theater, especially in Wasserstein's case, hinges on objective. Merging feminist "ethics with its aesthetics" (Leavitt 94), she values the artistry of her work in a way that feminist theater writers do not, and although her plays operate at times as consciousness-raising, she acts mainly as a chronicler and observer of her characters' situations, not as a propagandist who utilizes characters to forward an agenda.

The problem for me with Brown's definition lies in the absence of any remark pertaining to style. In itself, this may seem unimportant, but my vision of fem-en(act)ment includes a crucial reference to style because, as I will demonstrate shortly, it figures so predominantly in the development of Wasserstein's principal themes.

Dramatic style involves the playwright in both literary approaches and production values. Jill Dolan, for whom both these enterprises make feminist drama in general and "woman-conscious" drama in particular a matter of materialist investigation, has written extensively, for example, about what she perceives as the need for experimental techniques that undercut "the complicity of the representational apparatus in maintaining sexual difference" (*Spectator* 101).

Since fem-en(act)ment includes textual *or* performance drama, the definition's reference to style *can* address methodology for either medium. Regardless of which approach one chooses to examine, however, drama as an object of study presents problems not associated with other literary genres. As Gayle Austin writes, its intrusive stage directions and speaker cues make it "more difficult than fiction or poetry to read on the page," and live performances of it are "temporal, yet, unlike films and video, not convenient to study in detail" (*Feminist Theories* 2). In Wasserstein's case, the performance dilemma is resolved in two instances by video versions of both *The Heidi Chronicles*, originally telecast by TNT in October 1995, and *Uncommon Women and Others*, presented with most of its original cast members in May 1978, by the PBS Great Performances series.

Although I have seen these presentations and have also attended live performances of all of Wasserstein's major plays except *Isn't It Romantic*, Wasserstein's commitment to and development of her themes convince me that a study of textual drama, rather than performance drama, provides the more appropriate forum for intensive scrutiny. As Austin observes, "the written text … remains after performance is forgotten. It is what 'becomes' of the play, what the play 'means' to succeeding generations" (*Feminist Theories* 3).

The literary style that informs Wasserstein's textual drama and contributes to her thematic development *and redevelopment* reflects what feminist studies identify as a female, if not feminist, mode of writing.

## WASSERSTEIN'S LITERARY STYLE

As Audre Lorde once observed, the "master's tools will never dismantle the master's house" (110). This pithy and insightful statement applies not only to racial and feminist issues in general, as Lorde intended it to, but also to the place of women in a literary canon that still relegates women's writing to token representation. In other words, as Sue-Ellen Case wrote in 1988, women writers and critics should "abandon traditional patriarchal values embedded in prior notions of form, practice and audience response in order to construct new critical models and methodologies for the drama that would accommodate the presence of women in the art, support their liberation from cultural fictions of the female gender and deconstruct the valorization of the male gender" (*Feminism and Theater* 114–15). Although critics could argue that Wasserstein has not completely abandoned traditional form in the construction of her dramas, she unmistakably invests her work with certain literary practices that critics recognize as common mainly to women writers.

Speaking specifically about plays by feminist theater groups, Elizabeth Natalle notes that these works contain "non-linear ... techniques to convey the emotional and psychological development of the characters." Consequently, their plays tend to gravitate toward an episodic structure sprinkled with intimate monologues that, along with character interaction, emphasize the "emotional quality of the play" more than the storyline (61). As already indicated, Wasserstein does not write feminist theater works, but she does manifest an affinity for the techniques that Natalle identifies with such works.

Although Wasserstein's later works, *The Sisters Rosensweig* and *An American Daughter*, do not consist of a strikingly episodic format, *Uncommon Women and Others*, for instance, contains 16 scenes divided into two acts. The first and last take place at a 1978 reunion; the remainder recount in loosely connected chronology the women's senior

year at college; and—in a rather conspicuously nonlinear pattern—
an off-stage announcer introduces 13 of these segments with historical or observational material. Similarly, *Isn't It Romantic* includes a
prologue and 13 vaguely arranged scenes with seven prefatory "telephone machine" voiceovers, and *The Heidi Chronicles* comprises 11
thematically related segments spread over approximately 25 years
with a prologue set in a 1989 lecture hall at the beginning of each act.

Very little actually "happens" during these episodes. However,
as subsequent chapters will demonstrate, Wasserstein's characters in
*all* her plays do experience a psychological and emotional sense of
kinesis generated by inner conflicts that stem directly from the
changing climate associated with the women's movement. In actu-
ality, this sense describes the "drama" of Wasserstein's work, and,
except for *An American Daughter*, it typically evolves less through
event or action than through dialogue and the "multiple interior
reflections" that Rosemary Curb observes in "woman-conscious"
drama (302). Consequently, while Holly Kaplan (*Uncommon Women
and Others*), Janie Blumberg (*Isn't It Romantic*), and Heidi Holland
may or may not convince us that their actions amount to much, their
painful soliloquies leave no doubt that the inner turmoil hurts.

Like Jill Dolan, I prefer to attach the nonlinear, episodic process, along with its affective tendencies, to cultural feminism, especially since Natalle's association of its methodology with feminist
theater precludes Wasserstein. Dolan characterizes this approach as
a "documentary style," circular and frequently devoid of narrative
closure, periodically fueled with consciousness-raising, and almost
universally based on a variety of women's experiences (*Spectator* 85).

With regard to the last criterion, Natalle (114), Leavitt (17), and
other feminist drama critics invariably agree that the situations,
reflections, and resolutions found in women's plays emanate mainly
from the writer's own life. This is certainly true in Wasserstein's case,
at least to some extent. While admitting that she merely assumes a
persona in her essays, she muses cryptically that in drama, however,
"you can divide yourself into a lot of characters and hide ... in
different places" (Cohen 263).

She refers specifically to *Isn't It Romantic* as her "most autobiographical play" (Free Library 1995), and the lives of her three sisters

Rosensweig at times bear uncanny resemblance to those of Wasserstein and her two older siblings, Sandra Meyer and Georgette Levis. In *Uncommon Women and Others*, set at Wasserstein's alma mater of Mount Holyoke during roughly the same time she attended the institution, Holly Kaplan also evokes a number of similarities with Wasserstein herself.

As the ensuing pages explore, though, these plays also seem to evince the kind of psychological experiences that Natalle and Leavitt probably have in mind when they refer to the private sources upon which women's plays are built. *An American Daughter*, for instance, evolved from Wasserstein's ongoing concern for how the media deals with women like herself and, most especially, those in government who become public figures. *The Heidi Chronicles*, as another example, suggests Cathleen McGuigan, was created by Wasserstein at a "sad and disconnected" period of her life (77). Says Wasserstein, "I wrote [*The Heidi Chronicles*] because I had this image of a woman standing up at a women's meeting saying 'I've never been so unhappy in my life'" (Shapiro, "Chronicler" 90). "It was that whole idea of the We Generation, and then everyone was going off in their own direction" (McGuigan 77).

As Robin Morgan is quick to point out, the experiences contained in the work of women writers "are *not* ... private hang-ups. They are shared by every woman" (xx). While Morgan's second comment seems essentialist, Wasserstein's evocation of a dissolved communal consciousness in *The Heidi Chronicles* probably matches the sentiments of a number of committed feminists from the 1980s. The most significant aspect of both the private and autobiographical ruminations, however, is that in Wasserstein's case they operate in *all* of her plays as a distinctive twist of style, specifically by fleshing her character development more intentionally and then underscoring the psychoemotional nature of the characters' monologues and dialogues.

Wasserstein defuses the intensity of this undertaking, though, by incorporating liberal doses of humor into all of her plays. In a large sense, this, too, reflects an autobiographical disposition. "I think [humor's] sort of how I get by," she says. One, it "makes [me] entertaining [to other people], two it deflects, and also it's a way of commenting on things. So ... it's very important to me" (Cohen 265). Given Wasserstein's propensity for gleaning material from her own life and given the importance attached to this as a stylistic enterprise, she unsurprisingly, then, claims to create her plays principally "in terms of the rhythm of theatrical comedy" (Cohen 259).

According to Howard Stein, however, Wasserstein's humorous design resonates with an aura of "dark comedy and black humor," which, although it "reflect[s] and illuminate[s] the tragic condition" of her characters, also camouflages their misery (25). Wasserstein does not deny this. A "lot of comedy is deflection," she says. "If you look at *Isn't It Romantic*, Janie Blumberg is *always* funny, so as not to say what she feels" (Cohen 259).

Most crucial to her use of humor, however, is that Wasserstein effects an underlying feminist control of it. According to Lisa Merrill, the "point-of-view represented in feminist comedy ... affirms women's experience, rather than denigrating it" (275). Blumberg, in particular, exemplifies Merrill's drift. Janie's self-deprecating humor pervades *Isn't It Romantic*, but, instead of undermining her, it always illuminates her self-worth. "I could marry the pervert who's staring at us," she says to Harriet Cornwall in Act One. Instead of turning this into a desperate joke about her marriage prospects, however, Janie adds quickly, "No. That's not the solution" (82), and by the play's end, she chooses not to marry her eventual fiance, Marty Sterling, rather than abandon her career aspirations. In a single stroke, Wasserstein executes a feminist twist on the "old maid" joke and concludes with feminist convictions intact.

Of all the strategic characteristics identified with feminist literary production, however, the nature and use in particular of what critics term a "circular" writing style not only emerge most frequently in discussion but are also very closely connected with the episodic, nonlinear composition cited earlier. In short, it extends the concepts of the latter to include a repeated emphasis of an author's themes without regard to conventional dramatic development. Based to some degree on Helene Cixous' notion of "l'écriture feminine," a cyclic tactic theoretically gives rise to a "distinctively feminine morphology" (Case, *Feminism and Theater* 34) that approximates writing with the body. As Sue-Ellen Case explains, a "female form might embody her sexual mode, aligned with multiple orgasms, with no dramatic focus on ejaculation or necessity to build to a single climax" (*Feminism and Theater* 129). Translated into the mode of textual drama, a circular form reiterates the same experiences and ideas, sometimes with a heightened sense of emotional investment for its characters, but rarely with one traditionally tailored climax. Although wary of its biological component, Dolan notes that writing "with the female body allows for ... [a] florid, stream-of-consciousness style that inscribes sexual difference as the content and form of cultural feminist theater" (*Spectator* 8).

Of all her alliances with so-called female textuality, the most compelling influence in Wasserstein's œuvre lies with this cyclic treatment of the issues most important to her. Themes and recurring motifs appear and resurface for sometimes similar, sometimes different, sometimes closer scrutiny. Mirroring Joanna Russ' "lyric mode"—that is, the "organization of discrete elements ... around an unspoken thematic or *emotional* center" ("Heroine" 12; italics added)—Wasserstein literally views and re-views the private impact of the women's movement, first on her "uncommon women and others" and then more microscopically on Janie Blumberg, Heidi Holland, the Rosensweigs, and Lyssa Dent Hughes. Consequently, more than any other device found in her work, her cyclic enterprise not only creates a feminine structural design but also facilitates the central thesis of my study that Wasserstein unifies the five plays into a cohesive exploration of the feminist condition in women's lives.

As this discussion makes obvious, then, Wasserstein demonstrates a number of devices associated with female and feminist writing. She invests much of her material with autobiographical nuances, exercises feminist control over her humor, and fashions a cyclic treatment of her psychosocial themes, sometimes through nonlinear, episodic strategies. With her emphasis on these stylistic measures and with her divergence from the existing terminology connected with women's contributions to drama, Wendy Wasserstein distinctly complies with the aesthetic conditions that fem-en(act)ment inscribes.

## Purpose and Structure of the Study

Having established Wasserstein's feminist disposition and her place in feminist drama and textuality and having positioned those within my own framework of fem-en(act)ment, I am prepared now to detail much more specifically how Wasserstein utilizes fem-en (act)ment not only in each of her plays but also in their collective relationship to one another as an œuvre.

As I stated in my opening paragraph and elsewhere, Wasserstein applies her feminist and literary objectives primarily to the cyclic rendering of the effect of the women's movement on human life. Technically, she approximates the original premise for *The Heidi Chronicles* by re-enacting the contemporary "history of the Women's Movement" in *all* her plays, but by providing mere glimpses into its political manifestations, she succeeds only in highlighting a few select milestones. Consequently, in practice, Wasserstein enacts a personal history of that movement far more successfully than a political one.

The real history in Wasserstein's plays, then, is the private impact of the changing sociopolitical climate that the women's movement generates in individual women like the fictitious characters of her dramas. In the following six chapters I explore the specific nature of that impact and, in particular, its recurring patterns: characters' reviewing newfound options and choices made available through the women's movement; their confronting its communal repercussions between mothers and daughters, between women and men, and between women and women; their dealing with the uncertainty of their "either/or" resolutions in a world in which "it's just not possible to have it all" (Brustein, "Extremis" 34); and the distinctive variations of these patterns at the different stages of female life passage that each play examines.

In summary, Chapter 2, "Wasserstein's Uncommon Women," consists of two parts and initially identifies the type of character about whom Wasserstein writes in her œuvre and that *Uncommon Women and Others* introduces. Entitled "'Heart and Mind Together,'" this first section develops a composite description of "uncommon women" by exploring characteristics that Wasserstein's protagonists share. The second part, "Fulfilling Potential: Where Am I Going?" is devoted to *Uncommon Women and Others* and details the early impact of the women's movement on a group of college students as they "challenge social roles" generally prescribed by traditional values (Susan Carlson 572) and review their personal and professional options for the future, a motif that resurfaces at other life stages in every subsequent play.

"Having It All: A Woman Is (Not) Her Mother" shows that Wasserstein's second major play, *Isn't It Romantic*, acts as a quasisequel to *Uncommon Women and Others* with its re-view of that play's issues and with its more microscopic examination of two other "uncommon women" who have now graduated from college. Because of Wasserstein's interest in the mother-daughter relationship in *Isn't It Romantic*, however, Chapter 3 posits their conflicting options against choices made or prescribed by their mothers.

"'All in This Together': Idealism, Sisterhood, and Other Dilemmas" predominantly probes *The Heidi Chronicles'* exploration into sisterhood and feminist solidarity in the female community and, in particular, into its emotional support or lack thereof for "true believers" like Heidi Holland. Given Wasserstein's cyclic overtures, however, Chapter 4 briefly revisits the communal aspects in *Uncommon Women and Others* and *Isn't It Romantic*, compares Heidi's struggles to those faced by her predecessors, and, in a nod toward the mother-daughter motif, analyzes her decision in the end to adopt a baby girl.

Devoted to *The Sisters Rosensweig*, "Of Life and Men" broadens Wasserstein's thematic cycle to midlife with the question now framed as "Where have I been?" Inclined to accept that the best sisterhood is perhaps achieved more reliably within family, Wasserstein mainly seems resigned in this work that uncommon women cannot "have it all" and, in particular, cannot simultaneously sustain a meaningful career and a successful, intimate relationship with a man.

Chapter 6, entitled "What Price Glory?", examines *An American Daughter*, Wasserstein's most recent play, as well as her most serious and most controversial one. Set against the political realities of Washington, D.C., and the media explosion of the nineties, it shows the expectations society forces upon women in public life, and, by association, the attitudes it harbors toward feminism. Though she recycles her usual themes, as well as the midlife perspective initiated in *The Sisters Rosensweig*, Wasserstein for the first time presents her heroine's crisis as a professional—not just personal—one, and reiterates more ominously that "having it all" still remains to her an impossibility.

The final chapter, "Fem-en(act)ment Revisited," recapitulates the study's conclusions and asserts that Wasserstein's plays collectively comprise a my-story of the impact of the women's movement.

Considering the feminist vision in Wasserstein's work, as well as the contemporary quality of her themes and the numerous honors she has garnered, I believe that a comprehensive and scholarly undertaking of her œuvre is overdue. Through this study, I hope to further the establishment of Wendy Wasserstein as a major playwright and to prove that her commitment to fem-en(act)ment succeeds not only as literature but also as an intelligent observation of both human and feminist concerns in modern times.

# 2

# Wasserstein's Uncommon Women

## HEART AND MIND TOGETHER

> The heart is the capital of the mind,
> The mind is a single state
> heart and mind together make
> A single continent.
> —Emily Dickinson, recited by Mrs. Plumm in *Uncommon Women and Others*

"As a playwright," says Wasserstein, "first and foremost you must be true to your characters" (Betsko 420). Resolute in this self-defined standard, Wasserstein develops in her work a series of distinctive personalities, each of whom emerges with a unique style of rhetoric, spirit, and subsequent growth as she responds, in particular, to the impact of the women's movement in her life. While imbued with rich detail and emotional integrity, however, Wasserstein's protagonists collectively possess, as well, certain mutual characteristics that also fashion a type of woman—"uncommon woman"—whose life and struggles the playwright illustrates.

One of the most vital aspects of Wasserstein's women lies with their not-so-ordinary class constituency, a point that clearly precludes any suggestion that her plays foster some universal portrayal of women or of the conditions—both monetary and social—under which they live. In an interview with Esther Cohen, Wasserstein describes her heroines specifically as "middle class, upper middle class people ... not Philip Barry people, but ... not sort of working class" (Cohen 261). The wealthiest is Sara Goode (*The Sisters Rosensweig*), a highly-successful American careerist, who, although she might be the antithesis of Barry's socialites in *Holiday* and *The Philadelphia Story*, lives in a fabulous London home "decorator 'done' with ... expensive chintz" furnishings (3). As a rule, Wasserstein's major characters do not manifest Sara's elegant or affluent lifestyle, but with the exception of Gorgeous Teitelbaum, who reveals financial setbacks at the end of *The Sisters Rosensweig*, most of them seem comfortably solvent and unaffected by the economic concerns that at one time or another dog most people, including the middle class. Significantly, therefore, while money and social class do not define much about them personally, Wasserstein's characters can and do consider whatever paths the women's movement has made available to them without the complications of fiscal insecurity that might inform the choices of those less fortunate.

Although early family backgrounds account somewhat for their socioeconomic status, these women evoke a middle-class identity mainly for other reasons. For one, as Thomas Kozikowski notes, they all have college educations (453), and while *Uncommon Women and Others* elucidates this point by taking place at Mount Holyoke College and at a private reunion of its graduates, Wasserstein's other plays reveal that "uncommon women" also have graduate degrees. In *Isn't It Romantic*, for instance, Janie Blumberg has a master's degree; her friend Harriet Cornwall, a Harvard MBA. Heidi Holland (*The Heidi Chronicles*) is a Vassar graduate with a Ph.D. from Yale, while Lyssa Dent Hughes (*An American Daughter*), a Bryn Mawr alumna, is both a Ph.D. and a medical doctor. In other words, Wasserstein's women are uncommonly intelligent, a fact epitomized in particular by Sara Goode, a Radcliffe alumna whom nearly everyone describes as "brilliant" (*Sisters* 23, 30, 31).

Significantly, Wasserstein's women have translated these stellar educations into interesting, sometimes lucrative careers. As Wasserstein says with ironic understatement, they all "have good jobs" (Cohen 261). Kate Quin (*Uncommon Women and Others*), for example, eventually becomes a lawyer, while Harriet Cornwall wins a new job as a marketing researcher for Colgate-Palmolive. Heidi Holland is a professor of art at Columbia University; Pfeni Rosensweig, a globe-trotting journalist; and her "brilliant" sister, Sara, an executive for the Hong Kong/Shanghai Bank. Lyssa Dent Hughes has an even more extraordinary resume: a nomination as United States Surgeon General to go along with her career as public health professor at Georgetown University and chief administrator for a large public hospital.

Though this profusion of superlatively successful women in Wasserstein's works primarily allows her to explore the particular complexities with which a prosperous careerist must deal in order to "have it all," the educational and career-driven framework also results in the subtle but unmistakable presence of self-empowerment, another vital component her characters share. According to Jill Dolan, since power, "sexuality, and desire have historical connotations assigned by the dominant culture ... that have restricted women's abilities to express themselves" (*Spectator* 81), these attributes have traditionally been associated in both life and art with masculinity. Not only does Wasserstein defy history by allowing her characters to overcome these cultural and sexist restraints, but at the same time, because her characters come "of age in the late 1960s as feminism was redefining American society" (Kozikowski 453), she also reflects this struggle through their collective ascent to powerful careers, compiling in the process a dramatic history of the emergence of feminist influence and its practical repercussions.

Feminism, however, did more than enable women to hold powerful positions. It also reshaped attitudes toward women's private lives and especially toward previously unquestioned matters involving marriage, motherhood, and sexuality. Unsurprisingly, then, nearly all of Wasserstein's characters are influenced by these revolutions as well. For one, they not only lead sexually active lives but, as Rita Altabel (*Uncommon Women and Others*), Harriet Cornwall, and Heidi Holland demonstrate, they also speak candidly about them. Pfeni Rosensweig—seemingly unconcerned about AIDS— makes no secret of the fact, for example, that she sleeps with the bisexual Geoffrey Duncan, and *Uncommon Women and Others* "contains enough specific sex talk to cover the walls of every women's lavatory in the World Trade Center" (Eder 48). In other words, Wasserstein's women claim the right not only to define their public *and* private spaces but also to *speak* publicly about personal issues previously considered taboo to conversation.

Though the casual and open sexuality of her characters parallels the transformation in contemporary mores, their attitudes toward more long-term commitments mirror modern times to an even greater degree. The "class of '69," writes Wasserstein, "had no intention of waking up from a marriage at forty-five, abandoned in a Scarsdale kitchen, with the kids in college" (*Bachelor Girls* 146). In keeping with these sentiments, therefore, several of Wasserstein's major characters are not married. In *Uncommon Women and Others*, all but Rita Altabel and Samantha Stewart remain single by the time of the restaurant reunion, and although Harriet Cornwall announces her unexpected engagement at the end of *Isn't It Romantic*, Janie Blumberg breaks hers. Heidi Holland refuses to sacrifice her career for marriage, both Sara Goode and Dr. Judith B. Kaufman (*An American Daughter*) have divorced their husbands—two, in Sara's case—and Pfeni Rosensweig seems either uninterested in a permanent relationship or passively resigned to not having one.

Some of Wasserstein's heroines also remain childless. In addition to Janie Blumberg and Harriet Cornwall in *Isn't It Romantic*, Kate Quin notes that not one person in *Uncommon Women and Others* has had children by the time of their reunion. Although, in other contemporary phenomena, Heidi Holland adopts a baby girl at the play's end, and Judith B. Kaufman undergoes in vitro fertilization in an attempt to become pregnant, the only characters throughout the œuvre to have biological children are Sara Goode, her sister Gorgeous Teitelbaum, and Lyssa Dent Hughes.

Though on one hand these circumstances seem to support Elizabeth Natalle's view that characters in feminist-guided plays "establish themselves as people first, and as mothers or wives second" (117), of far greater significance is that the personal choices of *these* women to form or not form families are tied to the demands of their careers and of the times. As Kim Hubbard observes, Wasserstein's characters "like herself, [are] women struggling toward self-definition amid ever-changing societal imperatives, to be a wife and mother, to have a lucrative profession; to do it all and look as good as Meryl Streep" (101). Consequently, despite their education and successes, Wasserstein's women exhibit, subtly or otherwise, a simultaneous mixture of uncertainty, apprehension, and weariness as they examine not only the "endless preponderance of options" (Stein 25) but also the limited solutions available for juggling them.

Speaking of *Uncommon Women and Others*, in particular, Wasserstein confirms that these unprecedented choices confronting her heroines do indeed make them feel painfully bewildered. "The play asks: 'Why are they so confused?' I want to *show* you their confusion. But it's not saying I have any answers" (Betsko 420). In effect, this sums up the state of all her characters, as well as the plots of all her plays, and the confusion she names derives from the impact of feminism.

For Wasserstein, the impact of feminism and the quandaries it produces have profound consequences, both positive and negative. "What's troublesome, from my point of view, about the Women's Movement," she says, "is that there are *more* checkmarks to earn nowadays. More pressure" (Betsko 420). "The women's movement, the movement that said 'Your voice is worthwhile,' is the only reason I feel like a person. But what still needs to change is that women shouldn't beat themselves up for their choices" (Hubbard 106). But they do. In fact, every one of Wasserstein's characters continually considers and reconsiders the wisdom of her decisions as she tries "to do it all."

Invariably, this process leads most of them to an ongoing either/or predicament that delays or compromises both marriage and their desire to have children in the face of other self-enhancing goals. As a result, implies Hubbard, Wasserstein and her uncommon women exemplify not only a cultural trend toward this predicament, similar to the way they show the burden of decision about career-empowerment, but also a trend toward later marriages, failed marriages, and statistically-increased single households, especially among middle-class and upper-middle-class women.

Though they prevail while negotiating peace with their professional and private choices, the uncertainties endured by Wasserstein's women create unfortunate, though not debilitating, vulnerability. At its most intense level, for example, Judith B. Kaufman yearns tearfully for the child she delayed having, Heidi Holland practically pleads with a roomful of other women that she feels "stranded" (232), and Sara Goode's "brilliant" and "hard" (34, 38) personality barely disguises her distracted self-consciousness. To defend themselves against this vulnerability, Wasserstein's protagonists frequently rely not only on humor, as the previous chapter notes, but also on the support of other uncommon women, who, as Chapter 4 will show, are sometimes undependable.

Contrary to miring herself in confusion, misgivings, and questions, though, every Wasserstein heroine still persists in her belief that she can attain total self-fulfillment, regardless of what it involves. Consequently, even though she might not resolve her conflicts, her perseverance fosters its own rewards. "Usually," states Dinah Leavitt, "the ending of a [feminist-guided] play shows the protagonists reaching some new awareness" (95), and with the exception of her characters in *Uncommon Women and Others*, perhaps, Wasserstein's women also experience some outer transformation or inner epiphany by the conclusion of each work. The truce that Janie Blumberg, Heidi Holland, the Rosensweig sisters, and Judith B. Kaufman and Lyssa Dent Hughes make with their dilemmas, for instance, appears to result on a subtle level in quiet self-acceptance. On a more dramatic one, however, it also results—with their feminist integrity still intact—in Janie's rejection of marriage, Lyssa's refusal to compromise herself for a nomination, and Heidi's adoption of a child.

"What's really liberating," says Wasserstein, "is developing from the inside out" (Betsko 420), a statement that definitively characterizes the evolution of all her heroines, despite their ongoing angst and regardless of their resolutions. More than just "endure," as Howard Stein concludes (22), each one assumes her own distinct risks and arrives at a better understanding about herself and her relationships with others, "even if that means," says Wasserstein, commenting on Janie Blumberg's broken engagement, that "she's going to be alone ... [and] sit in her apartment and cry every night" (Betsko 421).

Given all the criteria associated with Wasserstein's characters, it would be reasonable to conclude that they resemble a lot of women, both common and uncommon, especially with regard to sexual conduct and the periodic bouts of vulnerability and uncertainty that tend to be universal. Yet, the composite profile that emerges from reviewing Wasserstein's plays yields a *specifically* middle-class, well-educated woman whose personal and professional ambitions cause a unique rather than universal kind of lifelong struggle with self and others. *Uncommon Women and Others* introduces her and reveals for the first time the underlying cause of this struggle and the principal theme with which this study deals: the impact of the women's movement on private life.

## Fulfilling Potential: Where Am I Going?

All people deserve to fulfill their potential.
—Heidi Holland to Scoop Rosenbaum in *The Heidi Chronicles*

"Women, Where Are We Going?"
—the topic of Heidi's speech to the Miss Crain's School East Coast Alumnae Association

According to Wasserstein, *Uncommon Women and Others* examines the lives of "college seniors in the seventies who, faced with the real world, explore their feelings about marriage and careers versus their background in tea and gracious living" (*Bachelor Girls* 176). At one time traditional staples of Mount Holyoke education, "tea" and "gracious living" in effect sought to prepare young women for the more genteel activities and social graces they might need to manage the home of a successful Ivy League husband. By the late 1960s, however, these traditions collided with the messages of the women's movement and, as this play shows, scored rapidly expanding options with deep uncertainty.

*Uncommon Women and Others*, says Wasserstein, "is in a way about feminism ... filtered through the people who were participating in it at that time" (Cohen 268). Its presence persists unflinchingly throughout the play, both in the 1978 reunion scenes and in those set at Mount Holyoke. In the latter case, several situations indicate very clearly, in fact, that the characters know a great deal about the modern women's movement even in its early stages. They discuss Germaine Greer, author of *The Female Eunuch* (1970), for instance, and several of them take a women's-history course which requires the reading of Kate Millet's gender-war opus *Sexual Politics* as well as Betty Friedan's 1963 classic *The Feminine Mystique*, which dubbed women's domestic malaise "The Problem That Has No Name" (15). As Wasserstein notes, the "class of '69 heard what Betty, Kate, and Germaine had to say. There were choices to be made, priorities to be weighed" (*Bachelor Girls* 146). In short, they heard the message and they acted on it.

However, even in the midst of a course that advances the thinking of Wasserstein's feminist triumvirate, the young women sift through mixed messages that cloud the directions that they think feminism has opened for them. Their instructor, Chip Knowles, for example, still espouses to them the doctrine of penis envy, the Freudian theory that suggests men have physical and psychological advantages that women purportedly covet. "The only people who have penis envy are other men," says Holly Kaplan dismissively, but a worried Kate Quin, on the other hand, thinks it "entirely possible" that she herself evinces it (59).

At times, as well, Knowles seems to impart the idea that women's private responsibilities still prevail over their professional prerogatives. He tells them, for instance, that his wife, a full-time homemaker and mother who graduated first in her class from Vassar, "may be mopping with her hands, but with her mind she's reliving the water imagery in the *Faerie Queene*" (24), as though her top-notch education is not lost, still matters, and somehow justifies or mitigates the imperative to clean.

Additional evidence of conflicting signals in Knowles' course emerges in Muffet DiNicola's story of "this French dish" who, unprepared for her class report on Rosie the Riveter, receives a standing ovation when she announces, "you girls are wasting your time. You should do more avec what you have down here—*points to her breasts*—than avec what you have up here"—*points to her head* (25). After "two months of reading about suffragettes and courageous choices" (24), Holly and Rita Altabel leave the class in protest, but "I didn't do anything," says Muffet. "I felt so confused. I mean this chick is an obvious imbecile. But I didn't think she was entirely wrong either" (25).

Another agent of mixed messages appears in several pre-scene introductions provided in all but one case by a disembodied male voice. Loosely related to the events in the scenes themselves, the material for these voiceovers derives in part from the 1966–1967 Mount Holyoke College Bulletin and from a 1957 inaugural speech entitled "A Plea for the Uncommon Woman" by Richard Glenn Gettell, president of the college. Though they advocate challenge and intellectual growth for women, a number of these preludes dilute their effect with conventional thinking. One, for example, puts forward the familiar ethic of female self-sacrifice by proposing that "an educated woman's capacity for giving is not exhausted, but stimulated, by demands" (24). The most ironic of these segments, however, occurs against the backdrop of commencement exercises, where the last male announcer proclaims, by "the time a class has been out ten years, more than nine-tenths of its members are married, and many of them devote a number of years exclusively to bringing up a family" (64).

Essentially, this convergence of societal and feminist influence forms the philosophical center against which Wasserstein's young women struggle to determine the course of their uncommon futures. Some, like Kate and Leilah, translate their newfound options into tangible graduation plans, though not without terrible angst. Others, like Muffet, Holly, and Rita, remain unsure what to do with those options and, much to their chagrin, have no idea what direction suits their talents.

The only one who appears to know what she wants is Samantha Stewart, a prefeminist prototype whose cheerful disposition and unassuming manner seem so suited for the traditional role of good wife that Rita calls her the "perfect" (39) or "ideal woman" (54). Seemingly unfazed and unbefuddled by the choices facing her—or terrorized by them—she announces early in the second act her intention to marry Robert Cabe, an aspiring actor whom she characterizes cryptically as "better than me" (26). According to Douglas Watt, Samantha is simply a "born homebody" ("Holyoke Hen Sessions" 27), but as her self-comparison to Cabe suggests, she lacks perhaps the confidence or self-esteem she believes her friends possess to do something more than "be [Robert's] audience, and have my picture, behind him, in … the *New York Times*" (26).

If so, advances Richard Eder, Samantha at least recognizes her emotional limitations (48). A "little talented at a lot of things" (54), she says, "I'm not as strong as ... Kate" (38), or as "capable" as Muffet (26), or as "incredible" as Rita (54). However, while her friends seemingly respect Samantha's decision "to devote [her] uncommon talents to relationships" (54), this self-described mission still appears somewhat forced and desperate. In fact, Samantha sounds a lot like someone who feels plainly ambivalent or fearful for an uncertain future, and as a result, says Edmund Newton, she "opts for subsuming herself in a tepid marriage" (22).

Unlike Samantha, the others expect to capitalize on the currents of feminist consciousness with more independent and dazzling outcomes. In terms of potential, the most exceptional one of the group is Kate Quin, a Phi Beta Kappan, who says, "I have a stake in all those Uncommon Women expectations ... [and] know how to live up to them well" (56). Inspired by her extraordinary talents and by the newly paved options of the women's movement, Kate establishes her professional goals from the play's beginning and, with self-fulfilling prophecy, succeeds in mobilizing her resources into an acceptance to Harvard Law School.

Despite her focus and unwavering direction, however, Kate feels a harrowing incertitude about the wisdom of her decision. Like most Wasserstein characters, she worries about—and will experience—the fallout of her studious and business-like approach to private life. In fact, along with Leilah and Rita, she actually voices some of Wasserstein's own qualms about the "checkmarks" women feel they must earn against the promises of the women's movement.

For Kate, in particular, "everything seems so programmed" that she's afraid she will "grow up to be a cold efficient lady in a gray business suit" (55–56). This parallels Wasserstein's reservation regarding, specifically, whether "the purpose of all this [was] so 21-year-old girls can get MBAs" (McGuigan 77). As subsequent chapters show, this kind of periodic ambivalence replays in her other dramas, as well, usually when certain situations begin to overwhelm the characters and force them to consider not only the prices they pay to achieve their goals but also which goals are themselves worth the sacrifices.

In Leilah's case, this ambivalence begins to emerge when the drive to succeed as an uncommon woman leads her to unhealthy preoccupations with measuring up to Kate's extraordinary potential. Already feeling the imminent pressure of the corporate world's duel between the superlative and merely superior, Leilah observes that "Katies seem kind of magical, and the Leilahs are highly competent" (49). Locked in competition with the Kates of Mount Holyoke, Leilah frequently skips dinner and other social functions for "more reading" she must do (17, 31), and in an effort to distance herself from the Philosophy Department's comparisons between her and Kate, she surprises everyone by announcing her intentions to attend anthropology graduate school and to do research in Iraq.

For Muffet, Leilah's plans seem "odd" (48); for Kate, they indicate Leilah's attempt "to make [her]self exotic" (31) and to escape the insecurities she feels when threatened. However "exotic" Leilah's plans appear, though, she clearly represents Wasserstein's concern for the kinds of damaging rivalries that arise out of the professional opportunities women have discovered in the wake of feminism. "It's important," she says, "that there is not one woman slot that puts you all in competition with each other" (Hubbard 106). This, however, replicates precisely what Leilah experiences. In response to Muffet's and Kate's criticisms, she confesses, "I think I just need to be in a less competitive culture" (49).

Even Rita Altabel, the "outrageous Ms." (Beaufort, "Wry Reunion" 140) of the group, who embraces a feminist sensibility unequivocally, recognizes the pitfalls of unbridled career advancement to which the women's movement invited them. With no definitive graduation plans, she tells Mrs. Plumm that "hopping onto the corporate and professional ladder—is just as self-destructive" as getting married and giving up one's "self-support, [and] spontaneous creativity ... trying to convert a male half-person into a whole person" (65–66). She finds neither solution satisfying.

These fears about human detachment, competition, and corporate politics that Kate, Leilah, and Rita respectively raise constitute Wasserstein's guarded but evident materialist inquiry into the traps that women negotiate not only as they balance the private sphere with the public and the old rhetoric with the new but also as they adopt a male value system to which they unwittingly, perhaps, have become heirs. As Rita so comically asserts, if "you spend your whole life proving yourself, then you just become a man, which is where the whole problem began, and continues" (66). As Chapter 1 establishes, though, this inquiry retains the mode of observation, not reformation. Wasserstein and her characters still want the goods—and, consequently, regardless of their misgivings, not only do they resolutely maintain their feminist impulse but they also internalize the exhortations of liberal and power feminists to fulfill their uncommon potential.

Despite no prospect other than a nebulous intention to write a novel, Rita's refrain that "when we're thirty we're going to be pretty … amazing" (42) underscores this determination. So certain is she that her "newfound female pride" comprises "an untapped natural resource" that she spurns an allegedly demeaning position at a publishing firm and says, "I *refuse* to live down to expectation. If I can just hold out … I'll be incredible" (60).

As a contrapuntal figure to Samantha and Susie Friend, a "one-dimensional" stock character (Susan Carlson 571) who represents the college's fading social traditions, Rita operates as the class radical and principal agent of what John Beaufort calls "feminist newspeak" ("Wry Reunion" 140). She justifies her own sexual freedom and "conquest," for example, as a revolt against "being … programmed for male approval" (33) and later complains that "everything I can name is male. When I see things this way … it's very easy to feel alienated and alone for the simple reason that I've never been included 'cause I came into the world without a penis" (34).

Like so many of Wasserstein's characters, however, Rita also relies on humor to mask the vulnerability she feels in the face of male prerogative. In her more "hilarious rush[es] of feminist anguish" (Newton 22), for instance, she ridicules male sexual banter by drolly mimicking it during one of her many creative "games," and in another scene deadpans that "all men should be forced to menstruate." "The only problem," she says, "is that some … schmuck would write about it for the *Village Voice* and he would become the new expert on women's inner life" (37).

The primary source of Rita's vulnerability, however, derives from the same "mixture of hope and apprehension" (Kozikowski 454) that they all feel. For her and Holly, though, this confusing state has different repercussions than it does for the others. In fact, as Wasserstein observes, the play in many respects centers mainly on them. It "examines the fact," she says, "that the Women's Movement has had answers for the Kates of the world (she becomes a lawyer), or the Samanthas (she gets married). But for the creative people, a movement can't provide answers" (Betsko 424).

Although Rita dreams vaguely of writing a novel and finding a "Leonard Woolf" (11, 69) to support and inspire her, Holly has even less vision. According to Wasserstein, "Holly..., autobiographically, is closest to me" (Betsko 424), a statement reinforced by the fact that the playwright herself had not even the faintest sense of direction after finishing college. As she told her audience in a commencement address at Mount Holyoke in May 1990, "I immediately spilled beer all over" someone on the night before her graduation when he had asked what she planned to do. "Frankly, I had no idea what was to become of me."

Like Rita, Holly defuses her insecurities with humor, although her less caustic wit and general warmth make her, says Douglas Watt, "the most appealing" of the play's characters ("Holyoke Hen Sessions" 27). Lacking self-confidence in both her academic life and her relationships with men, Holly tells Leilah that "[s]ometimes I want to clean up my desk and go out and say, 'Respect me; I'm a respectable grown-up,' and other times I just want to jump into a paper bag and shake and bake myself to death" (36).

Like Wasserstein, who did not feel "especially happy" at Mount Holyoke (Barney 54), Holly's "strongest attachments [are] to [her] women friends" ("Chic Love" 116), even though she also feels undistinguished alongside them. Her best hopes for the future, she thinks, hinge on "living through [someone else's] accomplishments" (40), a prospect that confounds and disconcerts the success-bound Kate. Though sexually active, Holly has no one special in her life to fulfill that dream, a situation that plagues her trademark insecurity enough to result in desperate phone calls and what Wasserstein characterizes as one "very raw" monologue (Cohen 267) to a Minneapolis doctor met during a museum excursion with Muffet.

According to Alma Cuervo, who played Holly in the original

production, "Holly is one of the people Rita talks about who will be pretty amazing; it will just take her a little longer" (Gates 5), a prescient observation, as it turns out. In the curtain-call coda that Wasserstein added to the 1994 revival of the play, Muffet as the class "scribe" for their alumnae magazine writes that Holly has just completed "her second book, *Gracious Living: Educating Women from Emily Dickinson to Hillary Rodham Clinton*" (unpublished ms. 78).

Like Holly, Muffet has not a single concrete plan by graduation, plaintively telling Mrs. Plumm, the group's housemother, "I'm assuming something is going to happen to me" (65). Presumably because of her overnights with an Ivy Leaguer whom she unceremoniously calls "Pink Pants" (50), Muffet appears in the play less often than Samantha, Kate, Rita, and Holly and therefore seems— like Leilah—a little less developed than they are. What does emerge clearly about her, however, is that despite exploring women's studies and the groundwork that feminism has laid for her to fulfill her potential, Muffet still very much desires the traditional security of marriage. "I suppose this is not a very impressive sentiment," she says, "but I would really like to meet my prince" (25). Asking Samantha why "I haven't met my Heathcliff yet" (26), Muffet knows, however, that even though she acts like a fool for him sometimes, the noncommittal "Pink Pants" will not become that prince.

Other students who also appear intermittently include minor characters Susie Friend and Carter. According to Wasserstein, "Susie Friend was a device. If you see 'Uncommon Women' as a spectrum of women: on one end, there's Susie Friend, and on the other, there's Carter, the intellectual" (Betsko 423). Reminiscent of the "archetypes rather than realistic personalities" found in feminist theatre groups (Natalle 90), they operate, therefore, as contrasting measures for the options facing the other women. Susie, a saccharine personality who induced Richard Eder to call her a "comic cartoon" (48), seems at the one extreme largely unfazed by feminist consciousness and acts principally as a "booster for outmoded college traditions" (Kozikowski 454). At the other extreme, the catatonic Carter, who functions in the play mainly as a "sounding board or wailing wall against which others can reveal their sins and neuroses" (O'Connor, "TV Tonight" C24), effects the aura of a "stereotypical genius" (Kozikowski 454) who will exceed even the most uncommon expectations.

Modeled on a Mount Holyoke housemother named Camilla Peach (Albright), another minor character who appears in the play is Mrs. Plumm, who, according to Douglas Watt's somewhat limited observation, only "emphasize[s] the school's principles" ("Holyoke Hen Sessions" 27). On the contrary, however, Mrs. Plumm also operates, like Susie and Carter, as a device, specifically as one of two that, in part, serve to anchor the structure of Wasserstein's work.

In this instance, Mrs. Plumm's small speeches secure the beginning, middle, and end of the play by framing the conditions of societal change that contribute to the "'massive insecurity'" Wasserstein says the group experiences (Elder 27). Welcoming the students to North Stimson Hall early in Act One, for example, Mrs. Plumm sets the stage for the play's principal action, the women's yearlong search for self-identity, with a quote from Emily Dickinson: "This ecstatic nation/ Seek—it is yourself," she recites (14). Although she immediately proceeds to reinforce the lessons of tea and gracious living that presumably will make them exceptional hostesses someday and seemingly advances some traditional female destiny at the play's midpoint by relating her long-ago decision to acquiesce to her father's wishes by simply marrying and teaching high school (47), by the play's end she abandons convention and acknowledges the uncertainties and possibilities wrought by the women's movement. "I have seen the world confronting Kate and her classmates expand," she says at her retirement. "The realm of choices can be overwhelming" (66). Then, despite her life as a "constant dutiful daughter," Plumm tells them that "I do not fear these changes," and with her own exotic plans to foray into the world, she reflects that even she—like the young women—has entered a "transition period" (67).

This "transition period," both personal and political, still exists when the women convene six years later at the reunion lunch. According to John Simon, since *Uncommon Women and Others* is a memory play about still-youthful people, "[n]othing much has happened to them" during college or by the reunion, "and what has is far from unusual" ("The Group" 103). What eludes Simon, it seems to me, is that the sociohistoric conditions against which the women consider and, in the meantime, implement their options do indeed make the circumstances unusual. Not only have they attended Mount Holyoke as it experiences the "last gasps of a generations-old policy of genteel mind-bending" (Newton 22), but they also represent the first wave of college women exposed to contemporary feminism and the "unnerving world of women's goals and options" that it unfolded for them (Kalem 111).

As the reunion reveals about the five women there, however, they still have not achieved a satisfactory truce with the conflicting lures of private and professional desire, even though they have, if anything, largely reinforced or maintained their feminist sensibilities. Kate, for example, has become a successful Washington attorney attending a "women-and-law conference" at the time of their get-together (8). "I've become a feminist," she says to Muffet (9), who herself has "taken a stand on birth-control pills ... [and] won't be manipulated by the pharmaceutical establishment" (9).

Nevertheless, despite "already [being] incredible," as Holly says (12), Kate has also begun to experience the cold efficiency she feared during her college years (56). Confessing to her friends that she feels "a little numb lately" (71), she can not decide whether or not to have a child, and she has just ended a relationship with a man who objected to her building a career in which her only time off falls on Election Day (70). "It never occurred to me in college," says Kate musing on her break-up, "that someone wouldn't want me to be quite so uncommon" (69).

Muffet in the intervening years has become "an insurance-seminar hostess" (9). Like Kate, she has paid a price in her private life for the demands of her professional one. "I mean, where [is] my prince?" she asks. Unlike Kate, however, Muffet feels a little more upbeat about her achievements. "I won't be in the alumnae magazine like you, Katie, at the Justice Department," she says. "But I never thought I'd be supporting myself, and I am" (69).

Professionally and privately, the others, however, have not fared so well as Kate and Muffet. The pregnant Samantha "guess[es]" she has a good marriage to Robert Cabe, but regrets that she has not "done very much of anything important" (70). Holly, still unfocused, has embarked on her third tour of graduate school, and Rita still entertains hopes of writing a novel, even with the apparently lack-ing inspiration from her would-be "Leonard Woolf," whom she married, she says, "to be protected" like Samantha (69).

Although Holly quips that she "hate[s] the women's move-ment" because of a rejection slip from *Ms.* magazine (12), she, Samantha, and Rita, like Kate and Muffet, still cling to the spirit of feminism, and even Samantha has tentatively explored the pos-sibilities of what Rita calls "really getting into women's things" (11). Through the reunion itself, though, Wasserstein also shows that they rediscover one effect of the women's movement, in particular, that they may have taken for granted. As Susan Carlson observes, *Uncommon Women and Others* ultimately reveals not only how fem-inism freed women from "the requirement that they bond only with men" (570) but also how in the wake of that it bred what Holly char-acterizes as the "comfort and acceptance" she remembers from the female community of her college years (71). Muffet concurs that "the one thing I miss in Hartford is having women friends" (9), and even Kate muses, "I don't think I appreciated women then, as much as I do now" (12). Without the foresight in 1977 about what their depar-ture from the restaurant really means, however, this play does not make clear what Wasserstein's later works—notably *The Heidi Chronicles*—make us realize: that the women will resume their lives isolated from one another and, as Chapter 4 discusses, unfulfilled by the promises of sisterhood.

Serving as the play's primary anchoring device, the two reunion scenes create a bookend effect, and in particular form a quasipro-logue and epilogue wrapped around a series of 14 "Polaroid" flash-backs (Kalem 111). Describing her episodic format, which Chapter 1 typifies as feminist-inspired, to be "an odd sort of documentary" (Betsko 430), Wasserstein deliberately inserts these first and last shots as a reunion in order to exercise a vantage point from which the women can evaluate the repercussions of their college years and the progress made since then.

Though, in short, the reunion reveals that most of the women "seem confused and unfulfilled" (Kozikowski 454), Wasserstein's coda added in 1994 suggests that twenty years after graduation, they have—for better or worse—negotiated their paths more clearly.

Living up to the uncommon expectations set for them by the combined forces of feminism and individual talents, Muffet, for example, has advanced to "Executive Vice President at National Colonial Insurance," and despite never having found her prince, she evinces little regret for not "juggling" a husband or children. Holly, as previously revealed, has followed her "best-selling" first book with another; Kate Quin has realized everyone's predictions for an exceptional future as "number two at Justice Department, living with number two at H.U.D. and raising two boys"; and even the competition-shy Leilah, who, Muffet reveals at the 1978 reunion, had married an Iraqi journalist-archeologist and converted to Islam, "holds [a] Princess Palavi professorship in Middle Eastern studies" at Oxford University. As for the "Others" of Wasserstein's title, Samantha, surviving her seeming uncertainty at the reunion, remains married with four children, and Rita is "still in Vermont. Still writing her novel," and with characteristic humor, "looking forward to estrogen therapy" (unpublished ms. 78).

As the coda discloses, the women have apparently managed to balance, compromise, or ignore the conflicts previously experienced in the original play's reunion and flashbacks. Despite its optimism, however, I prefer to approach Wasserstein's new ending with guarded skepticism. As a pat summation, for one, the coda leaps through years of unknown grief and triumph, and secondly, it appears only as a brief, fact-infused alumnae-magazine update. Given the opportunity to talk among themselves again, the women might reveal to one another—as they do during their private reunion—reservations or disappointments in their lives that would not find their way into a class publication. To warn against a too rosy picture, in fact, Muffet concludes the coda not only by stating, "Please write me with any news. I'm willing to lie," but also by altering Rita's refrain to "'When we're *fifty* we're going to be pretty … amazing" (unpublished ms. 79; italics added).

Ultimately, Wasserstein says she does not "know what actually *happens* in [this] play," but her working vision of "women sitting around talking," at least on a simple level, sums up both its drift and rhythm (Betsko 430, 419). As Chapter 1 establishes, nothing much seems to occur in a feminist-inspired play like this one, but true to

Wasserstein's inception of *Uncommon Women and Others* as something in which "women's voices could be heard" (Betsko 426), it is, according to Sue-Ellen Case, a "familiar example" of feminist drama that foregrounds experiences which "had never before been staged" (*Feminism and Theater* 67). As Ellen Parker, who played Muffet in the original production, remembers, "the play allowed women to talk about themselves" and the circumstances affecting them in a manner that few, if anyone, could remember in plays prior to it. "It was," she says, "an exciting shock to see all of these smart, funny women going on about themselves in this way" (Gates 40).

In reality, though, they do more than talk. As Howard Stein notes, these characters "laugh and cry and joke and love and hate and hug and kiss and smile and touch and play and work, everything that common people do ... while waiting for Godot" (22). In this case, however, Godot materializes much more specifically into the heady, yet terrifying fortunes made possible by the women's movement; far from being "common," the journey undertaken by feminism's first wave of college graduates into an uncharted future produces, as Janie Blumberg, Heidi Holland, the Rosensweigs, and Lyssa Dent Hughes later demonstrate, a woman and state of being forever uncommon.

# 3

# Having It All:
# A Woman Is
# (Not) Her Mother

"[H]aving it all"? Harriet, that's just your generation's fantasy.
—Lillian Cornwall to her daughter in *Isn't It Romantic*

A woman *is* her mother.
That's the main thing.
—Anne Sexton, "Housewife"

*Isn't It Romantic* provides the first glimpse into Wasserstein's propensity toward a feminist-inspired cyclic style of writing and, more specifically, toward re-viewing issues and themes raised in her previous plays. In this case, observes Michiko Kakutani, *Isn't It Romantic* virtually "takes up where ... *Uncommon Women and Others* ... left off" (C9) and resumes Wasserstein's primary and recurring examination into the impact of the women's movement on private life, and, in particular, into the same confusions regarding career, marriage, and motherhood that troubled her characters in the preceding play. Presented four years after *Uncommon Women and Others* and revised in 1983, *Isn't It Romantic* shifts its perspective significantly, however, from the more comfortable perch of campus life, where feminist ideals are mostly *debated*, to the more challenging world of two 28-year-old women, who must not only get on with their lives but also deal with the "emotional static" of others' expectations (Kakutani C9).

Although Wasserstein centers her play on two longtime friends, Janie Blumberg and Harriet Cornwall, *Isn't It Romantic* primarily "focus[es] on the emotional growth of Janie" (Moritz 612). Unlike her predecessors in *Uncommon Women and Others*, Janie does not talk about feminism per se or its relationship to the decisions she must make, but Wasserstein consistently dramatizes—sometimes subtly, sometimes overtly—that at both a philosophical and realistic level, it has influenced Janie profoundly. While Janie modestly demonstrates this influence by rebutting Marty Sterling's unflattering comment on women doctors as "extremely disturbing and discriminatory" (98), for instance, the most crucial indication of feminism's impact on her emerges as she attempts to situate its practical repercussions in her personal life.

Armed with a master's degree and a new apartment, Janie conveys—conceptually, even if not physically—the image of a modern, independent, "uncommon woman," who expects to fulfill career ambitions that prefeminist women twenty years her senior rarely imagined. Specifically, she hopes to become a writer, but, like Holly Kaplan and Rita Altabel, she does not know yet how to channel her talent into something meaningful. In the midst of trying to jumpstart her career, however, Janie begins a serious relationship with Marty Sterling, a wealthy young physician whose notions about marriage and motherhood collide with Janie's feminist ideals. Though Wasserstein does not actually name it, Marty's vision for Janie essentially looks like the "feminine mystique," the fundamental lifestyle—and, prior to the women's movement, practically the only one—which, according to Betty Friedan, "defined women solely in terms of their relation to men as wives, mothers and homemakers" (*Second Stage* 27). Although it takes her until the end of the play to make a decision, Janie eventually resists the efforts of both her parents and Marty to lure her, even when it begins to seem remotely attractive, into the thinly veiled "feminine mystique," which ultimately contradicts Janie's conviction that "dependency" is "not a solution" (82).

As Mel Gussow observes, however, "[r]esisting dependency is no small feat" for Janie ("New 'Romantic'" C3). At the onset of the play, Wasserstein characterizes Janie as "a little unconfident" (81), but, realistically speaking, this is an understatement. Until Janie undergoes a poignant metamorphosis by the end of Act 2, she

largely imparts a fractured sense of self-esteem and what Richard
Corliss calls "a rather complacent identity crisis" (80). "I have very
little courage," she tells Marty Sterling on their first dinner date. "I
am far too lazy and self-involved … have very fat thighs, and I want
very badly to be someone else without going through the effort of
actually changing myself into someone else" (98).

According to Wasserstein, Janie is "strong, but she doesn't
know it" (Betsko 420). Unfortunately, the fact that her friends and
family also do not know it not only interferes with her capacity to
make life decisions but also leads them to impose their expectations
on her. Equally formidable at times, Marty wants Janie to let him
arrange their lives together, the Blumbergs think that Janie has
waited long enough to find a husband to take care of her, and Harriet acts as the stoical voice—albeit a fraudulent one, as it turns
out—of feminist conscience and female independence. All of them,
in other words, read Janie like a child in need of guidance, and, consequently, they assume the role of mentor, advisor, or "mother" to her.

The biggest nag of Janie's "mothers" is the real one, Tasha
Blumberg, who Wasserstein readily admits "was modeled largely on
my own" (*Bachelor Girls* 36). Describing her mother, Lola, as "very
eccentric" and as an "Auntie Mame figure" who at one time went to
"dancing classes six hours a day" (Cohen 264–65), Wasserstein has
apparently recreated not just her mother's manners, interests, and
voice in Tasha Blumberg but also a few of their own mother-daughter confrontations that have in part prompted Wasserstein to call
*Isn't It Romantic* "my most autobiographical play" (Free Library
1995). Kent Black, in fact, locates Wasserstein's mother "at the core
of the struggle that gives her … work such resonance," an unsur-
prising observation given the fact that autobiography frequently
informs and intensifies feminist-inspired literature and arises in
this case out of the highly personal issues and emotional stakes with
which Wasserstein deals in her own life. "No matter how successful I become as a playwright," Black quotes her, "my mother would
still be thrilled to hear me tell her I'd just lost 20 pounds, gotten
married and become a lawyer" (154), a sentiment that Tasha echoes
almost verbatim during her conversation with Lillian Cornwall in
Act 2 (120).

Dressed in leotards and warming up to her Jazzercise tape, Tasha communicates uncontrolled energy when she first appears in the play. "I like life, life, life," she says. "I like go-go" (87), a quirky maxim that Wasserstein cites as one of Lola's favorite expressions (*Bachelor Girls* 16). Contentedly married to Simon Blumberg, Tasha has largely tailored her existence around the "feminine mystique," a lifestyle that she unrelentingly prescribes for Janie in the guise of "hav[ing] a nice life" with a "nice" man (120). "[L]ook nice.... Even when you throw out the garbage," she therefore advises (90). "[Y]ou never know who you might meet" (85).

When Janie first meets Marty Sterling, she wisecracks to Harriet that as soon as Tasha hears about him, she "will have the caterers on the other extension" (85). A kidney specialist whose father owns a restaurant chain, Marty, says Mel Gussow, is her "mother's dream figure of a son-in-law" ("New 'Romantic'" C3). Although she predictably does become obsessed with "the popover boy" (90), Tasha has lined up another potential suitor in case Janie's relationship with Marty disintegrates, a Russian cab driver whom the Blumbergs have known for five minutes and whom Simon will "take into the business" despite the fact that he "doesn't speak very much English" (105–06).

Although John Simon notes that Tasha is simply a "well-meaning but overnudging Jewish" parent ("Failing" 36), her quest to see Janie married never relents, even in the most unpropitious circumstances. As she and Simon prepare to toast Janie's new apartment, for example, Tasha cannot help adding, "I hope next year you live in another apartment and your father and I have to bring up four coffees" (89). Following this, in a hint-and-run response to her daughter's career prospects, Tasha points out that Janie's sister-in-law might eventually attend law school but only "when the children get a little older" (89), an interesting remark given the fact that Tasha has "just one" grandchild, but "look[s] forward" to more (121).

While the pressure created on Janie may seem exaggerated, Wasserstein reveals that in her own life the obsession with marriage and having a family overshadows in her mother's mind everything she has accomplished. "All that success intimidates a lot of men," says Lola (Miller H8). In *Bachelor Girls*, in fact, Wasserstein cites a telephone conversation in which her mother reportedly said, "your sister-in-law is pregnant and that means more to me than a million dollars or any play" (20).

According to Nancy Chodorow, a mother's primary "identification and symbiosis with daughters is more likely to retain and emphasize narcissistic elements, that is, to be based on experiencing a daughter as an extension or double of a mother herself" (109). This principle may or may not completely account for Lola Wasserstein's feelings about her daughter, but it does shed light on Tasha Blumberg's preoccupation with Janie's marital prospects. Tasha, for instance, has defined her own life so clearly that when she totes a new attaché case and calls herself an "executive mother" (92), she means it literally, even if not conventionally. Motherhood and, by association, being a wife and grandmother have become her "executive" position in life, but inevitably, no matter what the briefcase pretends to suggest, her "career" amounts to nothing more than a classic case of the "feminine mystique."

Because she has found a true "partner" in Simon, this "career" may work for Tasha, but bringing Vladimir, the Russian cab driver, to Janie as a potential husband-at-whatever-cost does not reflect reality or, most importantly, her daughter's wishes. "I want you to be happy" (89), Tasha tells Janie, but to demand that Janie opt as Tasha did for "a nice life" basically creates Chodorow's context of a "narcissistic … extension or double" of self. Janie wants more than "a nice life," however, and when she finally has the courage to define herself to others, she and Tasha will face off in what Gussow calls the "mother-daughter showdown" in the play's final scene ("New 'Romantic'" C3).

Unlike Tasha, whose crusade for marriage, family, and the "feminine mystique" amounts to nothing much more than a gigantic nuisance, Marty makes demands that not only bear very real repercussions for Janie's future but also reflect his own diehard values and unwavering self-interest. Noting his—and everyone else's—tendency to become Janie's "mother," Benedict Nightingale describes Marty as "a parent camouflaged as a lover, a symptom of [Janie's] real problem, which is an umbilical cord as thick and strongly-shackled as a ship's cable" (H2). While I agree completely with

Nightingale's estimation, especially as it applies to Janie's seemingly dependent nature, it seems to me that Marty would try to assume the same parent/lover role—if he could get away with it—no matter whom he dated. With his traditional, almost old-fashioned view of the world, he has an unswerving resolve to live in Brooklyn, where childhood memories of Jewish life still appeal to him, and to find a wife who will unilaterally devote herself to the family, both of which he will attain by whatever luck, kindness, or tempered seduction he can muster.

Although his allegiance to Judaism would undoubtedly preclude a serious relationship with Harriet, whom he already knows from Harvard, Marty feels too threatened by Harriet and incapable of manipulating her or anyone like her to achieve his dreams. "She's not sweet, like you," he tells Janie (97). "She's like those medical-school girls. They're nice but they'd bite your balls off" (98). Janie, on the other hand, strikes him as more "attainable" (83), a characterization that I read to mean not just more "congenial" but also more "malleable." Janie, in this case, becomes a prize, a witty, educated woman in the feminist era whom he can love *and* maneuver into compromising her own hopes in order to fulfill his.

Although Wasserstein admits that Marty "isn't right" for Janie, she characterizes him as "a nice man" (Betsko 420–21), an observation with which most people—certainly the characters in the play—would agree. I'm a little hesitant to dispute Wasserstein, of course, especially since Marty's apparent dedication to humane medical practice and his obvious affection for his father make him at least somewhat appealing. Though he also seems to care genuinely for Janie, Marty nonetheless wants to control her as well, and to do so he uses amiable prodding or direct ultimatum, both very disturbing.

At times, Marty reminds me improbably of Paul Stuart, the "sadist vice president at Colgate-Palmolive" (129), with whom Harriet has an affair and whom Marty describes—ironically—as the "least gracious man [he] ever met" (128). Paul, who refers to Harriet as "Beauty," sets the parameters for their rendezvous strictly at his own convenience, which eliminates weekends and overnights and otherwise depends largely on his ability to deceive his live-in lover into thinking he's doing their laundry. When Harriet rebels against Paul's arrangements, he makes her feel guilty by accusing her of not "deal[ing] from strength" (112).

Marty's nature bears little resemblance to Paul's insidious personality, but, like Paul, he does have a maddeningly selfish streak that unconsciously disregards or assumes what Janie might want while rather consciously planning for what he himself wants. For example, without ever consulting Janie, he not only rents a Brooklyn apartment for the two of them but also later makes arrangements, again without prior discussion, to move her there. Like Harriet, Janie sometimes balks at these scenarios, but, like Paul, Marty derails objections by making her feel guilty and specifically, in one case, by saying that she does not "love [him] enough" (139).

The first intimations of Marty's shortcomings actually occur early in the play. Although Janie does not openly object, she seems perplexed and uncomfortable during their first dinner-date, when he addresses her by the incredibly child-like name of "Monkey." Although she finds the endearment troubling, Janie is stirred by his affection for her, and, as a result, she fails altogether to realize the implications of what it might mean when he says, "Be sweet. I need attention. A great deal of attention" (98). As she gradually discovers, he wants more than he has a right to expect: an undivided loyalty that situates his own needs at the forefront of their relationship.

The most disquieting aspect of Marty, however, lies in the series of ultimatums that he periodically issues to motivate Janie and that Wasserstein writes in her trademark "either … or" formula that she recycles and re-views in *The Heidi Chronicles*. When Janie first hears about the Brooklyn apartment in Act 1 and seems on the edge of wavering, Marty tells her, "either you want to be with me—you don't have to; you should just want to—or, if you don't want to, then we should just forget it." This is an obvious attempt to control not only their relationship but Janie's emotions as well, and in a response symptomatic of her vulnerability, she simply says, "No problem" (110).

Smitten though she may feel, Janie never convinces anyone that she unconditionally loves Marty, but between her family's histrionics, her own fear of loneliness, and his urge to "move forward" in their relationship (130), she takes his ultimatums seriously at first and experiences an intense desperation about making a decision. Wasserstein, in fact, quite effectively dramatizes this confluence of external pressures in the last scene of Act 1, as Janie attempts to juggle Vladimir's unexpected intrusion, her father's unannounced visit, and Marty's insistence that she prepare an old-fashioned chicken dinner just for the two of them. Despite the scene's comic effect, Janie feels frantic, and her call to Harriet for an ostensibly quick cooking lesson actually reflects her need for Harriet's support to get through a suddenly stressful situation.

As Janie slowly starts to overcome her insecurity, however, she becomes more awakened to the kind of life she will have with Marty and his ultimatums. Worried that her career will "take over" their life together, he tells Janie that unlike his friends who marry women doctors, he does not want their children "brought up by strangers from the Caribbean." "I have nothing against your working," he says. "I just want to make sure we have a life" (129–30). Here, for the first time, Janie understands her future with Marty: he has the career, she might "work," and she will stay home and keep the family free of "strangers from the Caribbean."

Essentially, this scene illustrates the ramifications that can develop when even a "nice man" like Marty carves a relationship out of traditional gender roles. In this case, he not only disregards Janie's perspective but also willingly manipulates her insecurity to get what he wants. Wasserstein basically effects a materialist-feminist mode here, which, according to Sue-Ellen Case, frequently places "dramatic emphasis on the relationship between men and women and the necessity for change" (*Feminism and Theater* 93). In practice, Marty has been committing emotional blackmail on Janie, and it not only betrays an imbalance of power that seems natural and legitimate to him but also represents a conspicuous example of Case's—and Wasserstein's—point about "the necessity for change."

Janie, however, begins to understand that Marty will not change, and the last straw comes when he arranges to move her to his Brooklyn apartment without her consent. Angry with her demurral, he threatens Janie with a final mandate: "Either you move in with me tonight," he says, "or we stop and I'll make alternate arrangements" (138). By then, however, the "diapers are off" (Nightingale H2). Janie has, in a sense, "grown up" (Kakutani C9) and is prepared to reject Marty's role as her parent, lover, and guru. In their last scene together, when he berates her desire to "write sketches for a giant bird at two o'clock in the morning" and challenges her "to find out what it's like to take care of yourself," Janie at last realizes that to make him happy, she will have to make herself "a monkey, [and] a sweet little girl." The life she wants "isn't right for me," says Marty. "And ... it isn't right for you either." Telling him he's "not right" for *her*, however, Janie ends the relationship (138–39).

As Janie struggles toward self-determination against the demands made by both Marty and her mother, she frequently turns to longtime confidante Harriet Cornwall, whom John Simon characterizes as "her best *shiksa* friend" ("Failing" 36). According to Wasserstein's stage directions, Harriet "could be the cover girl on the best working women's magazine" (81). A Harvard MBA, Harriet wears "stylish business suit[s]" (93) to make her look, she says, "like a successful single woman" (85), one who expects to climb the corporate ladder of Colgate-Palmolive, where she has just secured a position in marketing.

Contrary to the "feminine mystique," the first impression that Harriet conveys with her intensity, "Bloomingdale's ... poise" (Corliss 80), and career fixation is its counterpart, the "*feminist* mystique." In response to the excesses of its "feminine" alter ego, the "feminist mystique" unwittingly fostered other kinds of excess and embraced a life in the business realm, which, according to Friedan, "denied that core of women's personhood ... fulfilled through love, nurture, home" (*Second Stage* 27). As a reflection of this, Harriet claims, in fact, that she does not "particularly want ... to get married" (101) and views Paul Stuart and any other available man as "fine" until she's ready for or involved in the "right relationship" (103).

According to Benedict Nightingale, Harriet's "casual amours and burgeoning career in marketing both seem to proclaim the independence she enjoins on others" (H2). To bolster the image she projects to herself and others, Harriet also has accompanying feminist rhetoric, of which Janie becomes the recipient when the subject of marrying Marty is first broached. Detecting Janie's ambivalence about him, for example, Harriet says women—and by implication Janie included—do not understand that "no matter how lonely you get or how many birth announcements you receive, the trick is not to get frightened. There's nothing wrong with being alone" (104). Janie may or may not have reached the point of being "frightened," but since she does admit that by 28 she always thought she'd be married and since she also halfheartedly jokes about insem- inating herself with a turkey baster, Harriet undoubtedly suspects that Janie has become alarmed by what Wasserstein calls "all these biological time bombs going off" (Kakutani C9). "I never respected women who didn't learn to live alone and pay their own rent," Har- riet adds as reinforcement. "Imagine spending your life pretending you aren't a person. To compromise at this point would be antifem- inist" (104).

But though Harriet lives and talks a life of independence and dedication to her career, she confesses to her mother that she would really like, in fact, to "have it all." According to Clive Barnes, this constitutes the central question of the play ("Funny Too" 70), and to a certain extent I agree with him. In fact, as the principal man- ifestation of the impact of the women's movement in *Isn't It Roman- tic*, it not only underscores Harriet's eventual actions dramatically but also plays a somewhat pertinent role in Janie's rejection of the "feminine mystique," particularly since she clearly wants to develop her *Sesame Street* prospects and to have a family life as well.

My point of departure with Barnes lies in just what to call the picture Janie craves, especially since she does not quite project the kind of intensity or ambition for corporate advancement conveyed by Harriet, in particular, and associated with "having it all," in gen- eral. For Harriet, "having it all" means that a woman is able "to be married or live with a man, have a good relationship and children that you share equal responsibility for, build a career, and still read novels, play the piano, have women friends, and swim twice a week" (133). Pointing out the impossibilities of gracefully or even neurot- ically achieving all this, Wasserstein not-so-unrealistically quips that the "real key to 'having it all' [is] not a marriage, or a career, but a very dependable housekeeper" ("Itch" 147) and a "zillionaire ... paying for it" (*Bachelor Girls* 127). The "whole notion of 'having it all' is ridiculous," she says (Betsko 422), and the "superwoman" standards that Harriet aptly summarizes do not, she insists, describe Janie's outlook (personal interview 1995).

What Janie wants, Janie cannot achieve through her own power, however. As Jane Eisner points out, trying to "have it all," in practice, "blocks part of what feminism is meant to bring about: systemic changes in institutions and relationships that help achieve a better balance between work and home. What have we gained," she asks, "if 'accomplished women' ... only mimic career-obsessed men, with no time for family or community?" (E5). Although "systemic changes" involve a political framework not found in Wasserstein's play, they undoubtedly inform Janie's unnamed frame of mind, which apparently lies somewhere between or beyond the "feminine mystique" and superwoman complex that do not quite define the kind of life she would ideally like to have.

"Having it all" does evidently meet Harriet's criteria for happiness, but what makes her blunt determination to accomplish it so intriguing is that she seems somewhat motivated by identification or competition with her mother, a near-legendary businesswoman modeled on Wasserstein's sister Sandra Meyer, a senior partner with Clark & Weinstock, management consultants (Wasserstein, "Don't Tell Mother" 196), until her death late in 1997. Characterized by Mel Gussow as "a self-willed tycoon and a feminist before it was acceptable" ("New 'Romantic'"C3), Lillian is an interesting role model to Harriet, whose promotion at Colgate after only a short tenure indicates that, like her mother, she appears to be climbing the corporate ladder quickly.

Like Tasha Blumberg, Lillian is also a "formidable parent, a svelte tigress" (Nightingale H2), who hovers over Harriet's professional development as much as Tasha hovers over Janie's personal one. "Don't say fine, Harriet," she says during one encounter. "You're a Harvard MBA. I expect an analysis" (94). As Harriet's mentor and a renowned corporate success extraordinaire, Lillian is the play's real "executive mother," so compulsively involved in her work that to fend off one of Harriet's recriminatory moods, she reminds her, "I wasn't home enough for you to blame everything on me" (132).

Yet, like Janie, Harriet seems determined to prove that a daughter's life resembles her mother's, if it does at all, only to a point. For Harriet, this emerges during the play's pivotal commentary on trying to "have it all," during which Lillian warns Harriet that "[l]ife is a negotiation." Suggesting that her daughter's designs are impossible, she says, "[Y]ou show me the wonderful man with whom you're going to have it all.... You tell me who has to leave the office when the kid bumps his head on a radiator.... I had to make some choices," says Lillian. "I had a promising career, a child, and a husband.... So the first thing that had to go was pleasing my husband, because he was a grown-up and could take care of himself" (134). Harriet, however, rejects the need for "negotiation," either because she does not believe that success and single motherhood have given Lillian her self-described "full, rich life" or because she has resolved to prove that, unlike her mother, she can successfully negotiate "it all": husband, children, a career, and a social life that exceeds her mother's steady diet of *Rockford Files* reruns.

Harriet's resolution to "have it all," however, does not explain why she suddenly and unexpectedly decides two scenes after this discussion with her mother to marry a man whom even she herself admits she hardly knows. Despite her feminist rhetoric about female autonomy and having an apartment of one's own, Harriet at 28 has, in fact, panicked at the prospect of being alone. "I didn't know what it would be like when Paul Stuart would leave at ten," she tells Janie. "I didn't know what it would be like to have lunch with Lillian and think I'm on my way to watching 'The Rockford Files' reruns" (143).

According to Wasserstein, Harriet's hasty leap into marriage, as well as Janie's reaction to it, is based on an incident that happened when the playwright was herself 28 years old. When one of her close friends had impetuously decided to get married, says Wasserstein, she felt exactly what Janie feels when—infuriated—she tells Harriet not to "force [her]self into a situation—a marriage—because it's time" (145). "I was amazed that I was so angry," she says while recalling the incident (personal interview 1995).

Janie, however, experiences more than anger at Harriet's news. Having just broken her own engagement to Marty, she feels that Harriet's sudden turnabout from "learning to live alone, and women and friendship" amounts to betrayal. "I made choices based on an idea that doesn't exist anymore," she screams at Harriet (143). Realistically, Janie's rejection of Marty results from self-growth she does not quite recognize yet, but her retort seems to indicate, ironically, that, although Harriet did not force her perspectives on Janie with anywhere near the same kind of coercion used by Tasha and Marty, of all of them Harriet had apparently exercised the greatest influence.

Though Janie's reaction to Harriet stems in part from the emotional bankruptcy she feels over her situation with Marty, her belief that Harriet has succumbed to certain internal and external pressures remains no less astute. Privately, Harriet might even agree with her, but Janie's onslaught nonetheless stuns her. Defending her decision against past rhetoric, she tells Janie, "I never lied to you. I lied to myself" (144). However, to justify the new approach to her life, she defensively suggests that commitment to a relationship poses a greater challenge to women than living alone.

Although this confrontation between Janie and Harriet seems to focus primarily on Harriet's insecurity and her immediate desire to "have it all" at any cost, it also targets the matter of female friendship and, more specifically, its failure to sustain mutual support during the kinds of crises women experience trying to live up to feminist ideals. As a subsidiary issue to feminism that Wasserstein only grazes in *Uncommon Women and Others*, the dubious reliability of sisterhood debuts seriously in *Isn't It Romantic* as a painful concern to which Wasserstein returns in *The Heidi Chronicles*. In this case, its repercussions have a devastating effect on Janie. According to Harriet, Janie's reaction suggests either jealousy or her wanting them "to stay girls together" (144). For Janie, however, Harriet's feminist ideals underscored—philosophically, at least—the decision to abandon a future with Marty, and consequently, Harriet's betrayal of those ideals makes her advice, in general, and her alleged devotion to "women and friendship," in particular, irrevocably suspect.

In a sense, though, Harriet also feels betrayed. Janie, whom she once called "family" (107), seems like an unsupportive friend at the very moment in which she gains a promotion, finds a husband, and in short comes closer to her vision of "having it all." In her defense, however, Janie not only recognizes Harriet's engagement as an act of desperation but also realizes that, despite Harriet's desire not to end up exactly like Lillian, she probably will. As Benedict Nightingale notes, Harriet seems so "in thrall" to her mother's "control of ... the business jungle" that her fiancé "will doubtless prove as disposable as her own father turned out to be" (H2).

Although Janie's confrontation with Harriet, like the one with Marty in the scene preceding it, indicates that she has begun to define and defend the things that matter to her, Janie does not recognize the extent of her metamorphosis until she finally faces off with her mother at the play's end. What precipitates Janie's proverbial last stand with Tasha is—improbably—a ridiculously undersized mink coat that the Blumbergs bring her for a gift. When Janie remarks with her customary wit that the fur would be "perfect" if she were "thirty-six and married to a doctor and a size three," Tasha makes the mistake of asking, "So why aren't you?" Provoked by her mother's insensitivity and furious at her inability to accept that she does not want "that life ... right now" (148), Janie finally summons the strength to demand that the Blumbergs let her determine what she wants for herself. Though marriage and motherhood, like the fur coat, fit Tasha "perfectly," they simply do not fit Janie now and, perhaps, never will.

When Tasha finally accepts that her "daughter is a grown woman" (147), Janie lets her anger dissolve into peaceful reconciliation not only with her parents but also with herself. Unlike Harriet, Janie ultimately is not her mother, but she does acknowledge—with pride, ironically—her mother's apparent influence in her life. "I'm Tasha's daughter," she says, and borrowing one of her mother's aphorisms, she declares her independence, stating simply, "I am" (151). With those words and with her solitary dance in the end, says Wasserstein, Janie has salvaged from Tasha's eccentric and sometimes overbearing repertoire the most important "gift from mother to daughter" (Betsko 425): the means, not the rules, to define herself as an autonomous woman.

By ending *Isn't It Romantic* with Janie and Tasha's confrontation, Wasserstein accentuates her claim that the play deals mainly with "single women and their mothers" (*Bachelor Girls* 30). While Jill Dolan notes that this motif is usually "paradigmatic ... of cultural

feminist theatre" (*Spectator* 9), *Isn't It Romantic* reaffirms if anything
Wasserstein's more holistic approach to feminist philosophy. As a
quasisequel to *Uncommon Women and Others*, in fact, it primarily
adopts that play's materialist disposition regarding women's choices.
After all, with or without Tasha's and Lillian's considerable influence,
the story essentially concerns the struggle—by any name applicable—
to "have it all," with the "important difference," says Michiko Kakutani, that Janie and Harriet are "not simply sitting around a dorm
room" anymore but living their lives and fast approaching 30 (C9).

Consequently, then, the play is not so much about mothers and
daughters but about two "slightly older versions of the 'Uncommon
Women' who graduated from Mount Holyoke" (Gussow, "New
'Romantic'" C3). Writing as if she had left the reunion at the end of
the first play to peek at their lives more closely, Wasserstein re-views
and reiterates not only the same complexities faced by her earlier
characters but also the increasingly problematic distress and distraction that co-opt choices and female friendships as women get older.
As a follow-up to that reunion, therefore, Wasserstein further situates the challenge against the sometimes overbearing influence of
mothers and others but most especially against the "feminist ideals"
of autonomy, corporate success, and "having it all" which have literally and painfully brought her heroines to the play's juncture
(Kakutani C9).

True to Wasserstein's creative integrity, however, *Isn't It
Romantic* is ultimately about character and, in particular, about the
emotional growth of Janie Blumberg. In short, the play's nonlinear,
episodically-designed scenes act like a "series of slides under a
microscope" (Dolan, *Spectator* 107), and gradually unfold the small
steps by which Janie advances from an insecure girl to the self-
confident young woman who respectively rebuffs Marty, confronts
Harriet, and asserts herself to Tasha in the play's final three scenes.
Having "stumbled into something [she] actually care[s] about"
(130), Janie in the end rejects marriage and motherhood in favor of
a potentially burgeoning career with *Sesame Street* and in the process
becomes more self-empowered than Harriet.

Although that choice might belie the dominant culture's value
system, Wasserstein as a liberal feminist not only defends Janie's

right to her decision but also intimates in the end tableau of her "dancing beautifully, alone" (153) that Janie has perhaps made the best decision. It is at once an emotional and uplifting finale, one that perhaps owes itself, in Wasserstein's "most autobiographical play," to her admission that "I'm the daughter who learns to dance alone" (Finn 366).

# 4

# "All in This Together": Idealism, Sisterhood, and Other Dilemmas

I thought the point was that we were all in this together.
—closing statement of Heidi Holland's 1986 speech, "Women, Where Are We Going?"

In terms of fem-en(act)ment, Wasserstein reaches an apex of sorts with her 1989 Pulitzer Prize–winning drama *The Heidi Chronicles*. Although she returns to familiar terrain in familiar style, she evinces greater maturity as both writer and feminist by creating a "minor epic" (Stearns, "Lively, Liberated" 5D) that spans a quarter century and willingly examines both the joy and—especially—the pain of feminism's impact.

According to Nina Burleigh, Wasserstein wrote *The Heidi Chronicles* "out of a personal sadness, a sense of being suddenly adrift herself" (1). "I wasn't married, and I was beginning to feel like the odd man out at baby showers," says Wasserstein. "I didn't know whether the sacrifices I had made were worth the road I was taking" (Hubbard 101). Though it appears that Wasserstein may have reached a crossroads regarding career and family life, what emerges principally from this reflection is that in pursuing options that others had not pursued, she felt profoundly alienated.

In effect, this isolation and its inextricable connection to the women's movement constitute the chief concern of *The Heidi Chronicles*. "I heard a lot of feminists saying they were not happy," recalls Wasserstein, "and that was the impetus for this play" (Barney 53). Specifically, it examines what happens when a "true believer" (247) commits herself to feminist ideals and then begins to feel "stranded" (232) when others—and especially, unexpectedly, other women— either do not share her views or do not provide the emotional support she had anticipated.

Chronicling Heidi's "intellectual disillusionment" (Linda Winer, "Real People" 7) is somewhat daunting, however. As Mimi Kramer notes, "Wasserstein's portrait of womanhood always remains complex" (82), but unlike that of her "uncommon women" and Janie Blumberg, Heidi Holland's "odyssey" (Hodgson 605) entails a quarter century of interrelated private and social transformations between 1965 and 1989. "I wanted to parallel a political life with a personal life," says Wasserstein, "to show how movements can influence a person's life" (personal interview 1995). This mission underscores the play's episodic chronology and its sometimes subtle tendency to highlight certain sociopolitical milestones, including, as Cathleen McGuigan notes, "key moments in baby-boomer history from the McCarthy campaign and radical feminism to the Me Decade and the rise of the Yuppie" (76).

Because the personal and political parallel each other so closely, the play's structure invariably underscores Heidi's development by chronicling those things that contribute to it. Its "moving snapshot style of theatre," typically used—as it is here—by both Wasserstein and other feminist writers "to chronicle [women's] disillusionments and disappointments" (Kramer 82), also provides on a much larger scale the quick and quirky review of general milestones between 1965 and 1989 that demonstrate Heidi's association with the era's causes. Yet, as the play traces these and "Heidi's life from adolescence to adulthood," it eyes more pointedly, as well, an accompanying "history of the women's movement from its early days in the 1960s through the consciousness-raising groups of the 1970s to the myth of the ' superwoman' who can 'have it all' in the 1980s" (Moritz 612), to—increasingly—the phenomenon of adoption by single women in the 1990s. At its most complex level, in other words, the inseparable connection and episodic weaving of all these histories— personal, cultural, and feminist—set the foundation for exploring the layers of Heidi's psyche and especially her unfolding sense of alienation from within the web of multiple political realities.

Not insignificantly, *The Heidi Chronicles* begins with mid–60s idealism. The most evident indication of this appears in the second scene, in which Heidi and others do volunteer work for Eugene McCarthy, who launched his presidential bid in 1968 on the one premise of ending the Vietnam War. By Act 2, however, nearly all the characters have seemingly abandoned their communitarian causes for the largely self-serving "rampant careerism" typically associated with the Me Decade of the 70s and the yuppie lifestyle it engendered in the 80s (Kissel, "'Heidi' Grows Up" 35). Heidi's closest woman friend, Susan Johnston, for instance, "transforms herself" in the course of the play's 25 years "from 'sister shepherdess' on the front lines of feminism to queenpin of the movie and television industry" (Gussow, "Heffalump" C13). Heidi, however, remains at heart, if not so clearly in action, an idealist, who "clings to her values long after her more committed friends switch allegiance from communes to consuming" (Shapiro, "Chronicler" 90).

Scoop Rosenbaum is the first person to observe Heidi's idealistic nature and to forecast, as well, the disillusionment it will cause her. During the play's second scene at the McCarthy campaign rally, he tells her, "You're the one whose life this will all change significantly.... You'll be one of those true believers who didn't understand it was all just a phase" (172–73). Heidi, however, has what Wasserstein calls passion (commencement address 1990), an uncompromising desire "to be a true believer and to live your life by something," even when others begin to vacillate or when societal values undergo a change (Rothstein 28). This committed idealism, which profoundly influences her private and sociopolitical ideology in general, serves as the underlying principle in understanding her eventual disillusionment with feminist friends and with feminism in general.

Although *The Heidi Chronicles* is, like all of Wasserstein's plays, "about choices" (Wasserstein, personal interview 1995), its combination of epic quality and character development changes the focus considerably. Influenced by feminist ideology, Wasserstein's earlier heroines basically sift through their professional options with varying degrees of angst and then debate whether or not they can successfully have both a career and marriage. Unlike her predecessors,

however, Heidi is much more affected by the sociopolitical landscape of her times, feminist and otherwise. Unlike them, also, she
knows at the onset what she wants to do with her life and she never
considers compromising her career for marriage.

Joan Allen, who won a Tony nomination for her portrayal of
Heidi, believes that Heidi was probably "raised in an environment
where her parents told her she could be whatever she wanted to be.
It didn't matter that she was a woman" (Rothstein 28). As proof,
Heidi defies seemingly practical and "political odds" (Wasserstein,
*Bachelor Girls* 89) and becomes a successful and self-supporting art
historian who never wavers from her belief that "all people deserve
to fulfill their potential" (181).

For Heidi, then, the crisis centers not so much on making
choices, as it does for her predecessors, but on living with the consequences of choices made early in the play, choices inextricably bound
with her eventual allegiance to feminism. She "gets in trouble," says
Allen, "because basically she's not a feminist. She throws her hat into
the ring of feminism, but basically she's a humanist," a characterization presumably culled from Heidi's own words early in the play
(Rothstein 28). Allen's observation, nonetheless, is still a faulty one.
Heidi gets into trouble precisely because she *is* a feminist, one whose
inherent tendency toward idealism makes her not only one of feminism's true believers but also the only one of Wasserstein's heroines to make that fact absolutely clear in both theory and practice.

To appreciate the dimensions of Heidi's experiences in this
work, one must understand that feminism does play a far larger role
in her life than humanism. Though her political commitment to
feminism does not occur until she participates in the Ann Arbor
Consciousness-raising Rap Group, Heidi in truth is a fledgling feminist from the very beginning of the play. In the first scene, for
instance, when boy-crazy Susan warns Heidi that she's "going to get
really messed up unless [she] learn[s] to take men seriously,"
Heidi—then a mere high-school student—declares that "there is
absolutely no difference between you and me and him" (164). In fact,
during the second scene, when Scoop meets Heidi for the first time,
he immediately senses her feminist bent, which she indicates during
a cynical exchange regarding 60s idealism (173):

HEIDI: What if you get left behind?

SCOOP: You mean if, after all the politics, you girls decide to
       go "hog wild," demanding equal pay, equal rights,
       equal orgasms?

HEIDI: All people deserve to fulfill their potential.

SCOOP: Absolutely.

HEIDI: I mean, why should some well-educated woman waste
       her life making you and your children tuna-fish sand-
       wiches?

On a subtle level, whether she knows it then or not, Heidi's school-girl statements—and especially that "all people deserve to fulfill their potential"—represent not humanism but liberal feminism's first principle of equality between the sexes.

Heidi's specialization as an art historian demonstrates on a rather concrete level, though, that the brief flashes of feminist rhetoric in these opening scenes are not happenstance. To illustrate, Heidi decides in graduate school, or perhaps even beforehand, to devote her studies to "images of women from the Renaissance Madonna to the present" (180). This lifelong undertaking might initially strike her and the critics as a humanist enterprise; but in reality, like all other cultural studies of women, it eventually hinges on feminist critical practices of deconstructing earlier icons created by male artists and of recon-structing women's contributions to the field throughout its history.

Neither consciousness-raising nor humanism, however, inspires Heidi to resort to these critical practices or to become a *feminist* art historian. Her awareness of the absence of female artists in her studies does. During her slide lecture in the play's first prologue, she notes to her students that "there is no trace of [Sofonisba Anguis-sola], or any other woman artist prior to the twentieth century, in your current art history textbook" (160). This is an undeniably fem-inist, not humanist, observation. Furthermore, the text to which Heidi alludes is probably the one she donates to Peter Patrone's hospital near the play's end: H.W. Jansen's *A History of Art*, a clas-sic work that Wasserstein remembers from her own undergraduate years for its omission of women (Stone 2) and that Heidi undoubt-edly noted for the same reasons at Vassar and Yale.

Consciousness-raising also does not teach Heidi how to promote her career as a *feminist* art historian. Although her participation in the "Women in Art!" protest during the play's fourth scene does occur after her Ann Arbor conversion, the nature of her professional expertise would have led her, just the same, to the "Chicago Women's Art Coalition," which sponsored the demonstration. Suggested by designer Thomas Lynch and director Dan Sullivan to coincide with the Chicago Art Institute's 1974 "Age of Napoleon" exhibit in 1974 (Wasserstein, *Bachelor Girls* 86), the scene acts as one device among many that allows Heidi the feminist, not the humanist, to deal with "ignored or underappreciated" women artists (Lipson 12), in this case, Marie Antoinette's portraitist, Elizabeth Vigée–Le Brun. Heidi the feminist also publishes essays on "art and women" (198); becomes director of "Women's Art, a group dedicated to the recognition of American women artists" (216); receives a grant for a "small show of Lilla Cabot Perry" (223); and plays an implied role in the 1989 Georgia O'Keeffe retrospective at the Metropolitan Museum of Art. In other words, Heidi's choice to become a historian of women in art is, as Karen Lipson suggests, one of the "more clever conceits of this clever play" (12), because by "depict[ing] man's exclusionist attitude toward women" (Gussow, "Heffalump" C13), it not only supplants the humanist potential with a feminist one, but also propels *an already predisposed* Heidi toward other feminist concerns, both personal and political.

Although her early quasifeminist rhetoric and art-history career demonstrate that Heidi's feminist disposition exists from the beginning and situates itself at the core of her character development, it does not really explain why a crisis develops. Confronted with this question, some critics tend—not without foundation—to link Heidi's dilemmas to the play's "powerful scent of autobiography" (Richards, "Life and Loves" E1) and to view her as "Wendy Wasserstein transmuted into a feminist art historian" (Simon, "Jammies Session" 66). Wasserstein does say that the play recreates "my story" (Free Library 1995), more specifically, the "history of me and my generation" (Rothstein 28), and, like Heidi, she campaigned for McCarthy (Albright), participated in feminist consciousness-raising (Wasserstein, *Bachelor Girls* 137), and speaks of adopting a child from China or Eastern Europe (personal interview 1995). As her reported remarks about the impetus for writing *The Heidi Chronicles* powerfully attest, though, the autobiographical impulse critics seize upon evolves not so much from the kinds of borrowed circumstances in her life that liberally sprinkle her previous plays but from an emotional continuum—from the personal sadness and general unhappiness with feminism that also inform the psychological texture and consequent conflicts of her protagonist.

To mark Heidi's crisis simply as a convolution of Wasserstein's private angst is to underplay the playwright's honest attempt to sort through the complexities of Heidi's commitment to feminism and "the expectations that were raised and then, for some reason, were just left hanging" (Rothstein 1). As Sylviane Gold observes, "Heidi buys the rhetoric of the first, heady years of feminism" (A13) only to end up questioning its direction during the play's emotional and climactic speech several scenes and 18 years later. What Wasserstein dramatizes in between is the chronicle she wants us to understand: not the fuzzy autobiographical center, but the evolution of Heidi's personal crisis within the social arena of feminism.

In reality, Heidi's problems materialize from a complicated web of intersecting conditions in the play. She is established in the plot's complex structure as an incurable idealist in an age of unenduring movements and as a closet protofeminist with academic interests in women's affairs. Her crisis emerges when the changing tone and unfulfilled promises of the women's movement collide with both her idealism and her emotional response to consciousness-raising in the play's third scene. Except for her soliloquy at the Plaza Hotel, this is, in fact, the play's most crucial scene, the one that pinpoints the moment at which she leaps from the personal to the political—from her private vision of feminism to the communal one. More importantly, "the way Heidi interprets it," says Wasserstein, "changes her life" (personal interview 1995).

As a tool for creating feminist solidarity, consciousness-raising originated with early Marxist and socialist feminisms, which recognized the need to create a forum for women to become aware of the conditions of their existence in much the same way Marx and Lenin envisioned the need for a forum to raise class consciousness among the proletariat. In practice, feminist consciousness-raising, then, acts as a materialist strategy "for correcting the distortions of patriarchal ideology" (Jagger, *Feminist Politics* 365–66) and as a cultural strategy through which women bond together and share their experiences (Dolan 85). In Heidi's case, both strategies prove seductive, and—as interpreted by her—they forever influence how she perceives the role of men in her life and the role of female solidarity or sisterhood.

Although sisterhood becomes the pivotal ingredient of Heidi's experience in Ann Arbor, it would be wrong to underestimate the importance of men in her life. As John Simon notes, "in this examination of how women, with or without benefit of feminism, adjust to their emotional-biological needs, men matter" ("Partial Autobiographies" 49), and in Heidi's case, there is "always an unconsummated relationship with some shadowy editor in the background" (Brustein, "Extremis" 33). These off-stage relationships routinely seem to fail because of the same either/or scenario that Marty Sterling creates for Janie Blumberg in *Isn't It Romantic*, not because of their irrelevance to Heidi or because of man-hating.

On the contrary, Peter Patrone remains throughout the play her closest friend and "soulmate" (Gussow, "Heffalump" C13), a homosexual who would otherwise possess "everything Heidi wants from a man" (Simon, "Partial Autobiographies" 49). However, as her decision to leave one lover rather than reject a position at Columbia University demonstrates, even in love Heidi's liberal feminism is steadfast. She simply and consistently rejects the condition of "either" choosing a career as an art historian "or" forfeiting it for a family life.

Despite some misery over her relationships with men, however, her consciousness-raising experience in Ann Arbor merely reinforces what the play's first two scenes indicate she already knows: that all "people deserve to fulfill their potential," that a well-educated woman should not have to spend her life making tuna-fish sandwiches for her husband (173), and that she deserved something better than Scoop, a man the critics universally loathe. An "irresistibly smug cad" (Gerard, review of *Heidi* 38) and "flippant womanizer" (Kissel, "Heidi Grows Up" 35), Scoop epitomizes a lethal mixture of charm and "horrifying selfishness" (Barnes, "Me Generation" 333). From the beginning, he "offers Heidi no choice but subjugation to his will" (Gussow, "Heffalump" C13), either as his mistress or as a "traditional wife, who stays home and stokes the embers of his ego" (Richards, "Life and Loves" E6). As Sylviane Gold observes, under the circumstances, one "can't help wondering why … Heidi would put up with him" (A13), but Heidi reveals the sad truth at Ann Arbor: "I keep allowing [him] to account for so much of what I think of myself. I allow him to make me feel valuable. And the bottom line is, I know that's wrong. I would tell any friend of mine that's wrong" (182).

What makes Heidi's consciousness-raising a turning point, both in her relationship with Scoop and in terms of her self-image, is not some newly-minted epiphany about her own potential, which she clearly knows she possesses, and not some spontaneous revelation that Scoop "can't cope with the challenge of dealing with an A–plus woman" (O'Connor, "A–Plus Woman" D18), but rather the realization that she's not alone. In other words, "sisterhood strikes [Heidi] as the path of the future: women supporting and celebrating one another" in communal solidarity (Richards, "Life and Loves" E6).

When Heidi first arrives at the rap group with her friend Susan, though, she "sits slightly outside the circle" (176) and is consequently perceived as an "interloper" (Kramer 82) whose "inherent reserve … manifests itself as causticity" (Richards, "Life and Loves" E6). Deriving Heidi's uneasiness from her own first consciousness-raising session in 1970, Wasserstein recalls that one person "simplified all political stances with one sweeping agenda. According to her, 'Body hair [was] the last frontier,'" with the "good guys … on the furry side" (Bachelor Girls 137). Echoing Wasserstein's memory of this, one of the women, a 30-year-old lesbian physicist named Fran, propels Heidi's involvement with the group by drawing the battle lines: "either you shave your legs," insists Fran, "or you don't" (178, 180).

What changes Heidi's initial demeanor rests specifically on the way the Ann Arbor "collective of lesbians, career women, [and] radicals" (Brustein, "Extremis" 34) deal with her and with one another. As the spokesperson against patriarchal subjugation, Fran exerts the ideological influence in the group by reminding them that "every woman in this room has been taught that the desires and dreams of her husband, her son, or her boss are much more important than her own" (181). Although this essentially sums up the experiences of several of the women, including Heidi, Fran's words alone do not convey the "terrible sadness and insecurity all [the] brave talk barely masks" (Gerard, review of *Heidi* 38). Jill, a 40-year-old mother of four, for instance, reveals that until recently she "had completely forgotten to take care of" herself while answering the demands of her husband and children (177). Becky, a 17-year-old whose dysfunctional parents have left her unsupervised for six months, has a live-in, abusive boyfriend. "I make all his meals, and I never disagree with him," she says. "But then he just gets angry or stoned. So ... I lock the bathroom door and cry. But I try not to make any sound" (179).

Heidi, it appears, is touched by the way Fran and Jill respond to Becky's horrifying story. "Lamb, no one here is ever going to hate you," coos the normally abrasive Fran, while Jill, saying that women "like us have to learn to give to those who appreciate it, instead of those who expect it" (179), offers to let Becky stay with her family. Although Heidi still feels reluctant to reveal her own problems with Scoop to the others, their reactions to Becky's unhappiness form the first impression of what sisterhood could mean.

Characterizing the meeting as a way for them to "reach out" to one another as "sisters" (177), Fran wants Heidi to break her silence. Presumably reticent because of the newness of the experience and her unfamiliarity with everyone but Susan, Heidi joins the group spirit only after Susan blurts out that "Heidi is obsessed with an asshole." When Heidi declares the matter "personal," she sets the stage for the feminist rhetoric that will change her life. "'Personal' has kept us apart for so many years," says Jill. "'Personal' means I know what I'm doing is wrong, but I have so little faith in myself, I'm going to keep it a secret and go right on doing it" (180).

At this point, Fran becomes the ideological spokesperson again, this time using patriarchy to encourage positive, feminist activism. The "only way to turn [sexism] around," she says, "is for us, right here, to try to make what *we* want, what *we* desire to be, as vital as it would undoubtedly be to any man. And then we can go out there and really make a difference! ... [But] nothing's going to change until we really start talking to each other" (181). Inspired by political possibility and the promise of sisterhood, Heidi does finally talk.

Calling Scoop a "charismatic creep" who "dates a lot of other women" and who stays "aloof" when "I need him" (181–82), she finds strength from Jill's and Fran's words and from the compassion witnessed with Becky to admit that she has allowed Scoop to determine her self-worth. "I hope our daughters never feel like us," she says. "I hope all our daughters feel ... worthwhile." Obviously refreshed by her confession and by the glimmer of hope she senses from her experience with the rap group, she asks if Fran will "promise we can accomplish that much" through the women's movement and its supportive arm of sisterhood (182). When Fran answers with a hug, Heidi's conversion is complete.

Afterwards, Susan declares their importance to one another, and, at Jill's suggestion, they join hands and begin to sing, "Friends, friends, friends/ We will always be" (182-83). Switching from campfire songs to more contemporary music, they end the scene laughing together and dancing to Aretha Franklin's "Respect," thereby "re-creat[ing] the euphoric spirit of the time even as it lampoons its inane, huggy rituals" (Gold A13). For Heidi, it is an emotional catharsis, the moment in which her once-private life comes into the fold of the women's movement and into a sisterhood of feminist allies, and the moment, above all, in which her incurable idealism makes her one of feminism's true believers.

Unfortunately, however, sisterhood does not quite turn into what Heidi expects. According to Bette Mandl, the consciousness-raising scene "evokes the images of sisterhood that had prevailed during what is now recognizable as a particular phase of feminism" (124). Having created it as a tongue-in-cheek send-up of 70s sensitivity groups that in hindsight seem less meaningful than they first appeared, Wasserstein probably agrees with Mandl regarding the images. In general, however, the importance of sisterhood itself to the play—and to Wasserstein—is unmistakable.

For one, she originally named *The Heidi Chronicles*—among other titles—"The Old Girl Network" (*Chronicles* notebook, box 3, folder 1) and steadfastly believes that the "signature of a truly enviable woman is the tenacity and continuity of her women friends." Nonetheless, Wasserstein in recent years has also realized, however ruefully, what Heidi does not: that although "female friendships are at all costs to be protected ... they generally, no matter how close, become secondary in each other's lives" and "move on" ("Beware Women" 82). The play's first clue to this is that except for Susan, the rap group women never again re-surface in the play or, for the most part, in Heidi's life.

Wasserstein undoubtedly suspected the inconstancy of female solidarity even in the 1970s when she wrote the reunion scene for *Uncommon Women and Others.* Meeting for a catch-up luncheon, the formerly close coterie of college friends have in some cases not reunited at all since graduation, and they make no plans to gather together again anytime soon—as a support group or for more catch-up—despite the apparent restlessness they have just shared with one another. They, however, seem prepared to accept the separation. Heidi does not. More importantly, although Susan remains in her life, she ultimately disappoints Heidi more than any of the other women in the play and proves to be the most devastating setback to Heidi's sense of sisterhood.

Originally caught in the same fervor of idealism as Heidi, Susan appears in Act 1 as a McCarthy volunteer and a seemingly committed feminist, who not only introduces Heidi to consciousness-raising but also abandons life as a law clerk at the Supreme Court to live "on a Women's Health and Legal Collective in Montana" as a "radical-shepherdess-counselor" (188). Unlike Scoop, however, whose life as a "dazzling opportunist" (Simon, "Jammies Session" 68) remains for better or worse consistent throughout the play, Heidi's "chameleon friend" (Weales 574) is swept away by the materialistic spirit of the Me Decade and the age of superwoman, and by Act 2 she transforms herself "from a mountain radical to a Hollywood sharpie" (Linda Winer, "Real People" 11). Having finished business school and moved to Los Angeles "as executive VP for a new production company" (209), she tells Heidi in their last scene

together that "I've been so many people, I don't know who I am" (224).
"Wild, practical, and fifty-percent rayon" (209), Susan "mutates with
the times" (Richards, "Life and Loves" E6), and for that reason, says
Wasserstein, "Heidi can't depend on her" (personal interview 1995).

Although Cathleen McGuigan believes that Susan acts "merely
[as] a foil" (77) to Heidi's development, I disagree. In a play that
examines disillusionment with the women's movement and, in particular, with the unfulfilled promises of sisterhood, I believe that
Heidi feels betrayed by Susan in much the same way that Janie feels
betrayed by Harriet in *Isn't It Romantic*. Like Harriet, Susan acts as
her friend's arbiter of feminism. Not only does she introduce Heidi
to the political component of the women's movement and to its element of sisterhood by bringing her to the Ann Arbor Consciousness-raising Rap Group, but for a period of time she also exemplifies
for Heidi the meaning of total commitment to these principles by
spending several years on a "feminist dude ranch" (209).

But in Act 2, Scene 3, which takes place just before the emotional speech depicting sisterhood's failure, Susan shocks Heidi by
telling her, "I'm not political anymore. I mean, equal rights is one
thing, equal pay is one thing, but blaming everything on being a
woman is just passe." Furthermore, she says, the current generation
of women does not "want to make the same mistakes we did" (226),
to which the stunned and confused Heidi replies, "I don't think we
made such big mistakes" (227).

According to Bette Mandl, "Susan has left behind all that
Heidi still believes in. She has moved into 'the system.' The sense
of betrayal and abandonment Heidi feels is precisely that of someone who had counted on family loyalty, the ongoing support of sisters, above all" (124). To worsen the situation, Heidi in this scene
desperately wants to confide her encroaching vulnerability and disillusionment to Susan. But Susan has other things on her mind, and
does not want the conversation to be "too deep"; and although she
adds that "I've been thinking a lot about you and how much I love
you, and I promise I have the answer for both of us," she does not
(224). In fact, she never truly attempts here to listen to Heidi or help
her, thereby compounding the betrayal of feminism with the
betrayal of their friendship.

According to John Simon, "Susan lacks Heidi's dimensions" ("Partial Autobiographies" 49). She "has just the cheerful, unapologetic bustle one finds in people who manage to get through their lives without ever reflecting on them" (Gold A13). Susan fails, consequently, to understand how seriously Heidi treats the causes they at one time shared, and though she confesses during lunch that she "miss[es] 'The Heidi Chronicles'" (227), Susan has little insight into the influence she has unwittingly exerted on them or the role she plays in Heidi's disillusionment.

Though Susan turns out to be an unreliable sister and friend to Heidi, she nonetheless reflects her times in Act 2 and reflects, in particular, the changes in the women's movement. As a successful Hollywood executive, she has become an 80s superwoman, affluent, fashionable, businesslike, and busy, attributes that Heidi, consciously or otherwise, has largely eschewed. As such, Susan illustrates the transformation of feminism from idealism to materialism, from gathering at rap groups in 1970 to gathering at power showers in 1980, from demanding equal rights to consuming the dubious spoils of victory.

Although the idealistic Heidi "gets left behind" by this transformation (Gold A13), other women in the play, and especially those who attend the power shower that opens Act 2, do not (209). In terms of both structure and character development, the baby shower given for Scoop's wife acts as a counterpoint to the consciousness-raising scene. Unlike the activist women who gathered in Act 1 as a support group, Susan, Lisa Rosenbaum, her sister Denise, and their friend Betsy have little interest in honest group dynamics or in personal revelation, as their reluctance to inform Lisa of Scoop's infidelity and her reluctance to admit it demonstrate. Furthermore, most of these women are well on their way to becoming macrocosmic superwomen who manage to have a husband, a successful career, and all the dreamed-of status symbols that accompany both.

Lisa, for instance, eventually becomes the affluent mother of two, with Scoop's considerable income as a lawyer and publisher of *Boomer* magazine and her salary as a prize-winning illustrator of children's books. Betsy, managing editor for *Boomer*, has already enrolled her unborn child in a "cram course for ... the SATs for nursery school" (208). Of all of them, however, Lisa's sister Denise is the one who, according to Linda Winer, especially "knows how to have it all" ("Real People" 11). "[O]nce my career's in place," says· Denise, "I definitely want to have my children before I'm thirty. I mean, isn't that what you guys fought for? So we could 'have it all?'" (211). Denise eventually does exactly what she predicts. Graduating from production assistant for *Hello, New York*, a television program hosted by another "superwoman," April Lambert, to story editor at Susan's Hollywood studio, she marries, becomes a mother, and plans for her girls "to get married in their twenties, have their first baby by thirty, and make a pot of money" (226). In all, says Joan Allen, "it's just a world [Heidi] can't relate to" (Rothstein 28)

Although, as Cathleen McGuigan points out, these women seem more like caricatures than real persons (77), as devices they represent not only Wasserstein's "picture of women who want [to have] it all" (Gussow, "Heffalump" C13) but also the "co-opting of feminist politics" (McGuigan 76) in which Heidi's dream about fulfilling potential turns into stifling standards of success or, worse, into "greedy narcissism" (Gold A13). More importantly, Heidi— unmarried, childless, idealistic, and not materialistic—can neither expect nor feel the spirit of sisterhood with them, and because "there's no group to include herself in" (Rothstein 28), she comes to feel stranded.

According to Nina Burleigh, the "idea of 'having it all' is distasteful to Wasserstein" (8), a point the playwright underscored during an interview with Cathleen McGuigan when she wondered if "the purpose of all this [was] so that 21-year-old girls can get MBAs" (77). Although she recycles the theme of having it all from *Isn't It Romantic*, Wasserstein nevertheless stresses that it "really isn't the point of the play. The point of the play is when Peter ... says to Heidi, 'You know, our friends are our family.' ... [It's] about a generation, about people whose friends are their family, and who never connected the way they thought they would" (Burleigh 8). This specifically reveals itself in the play as failed sisterhood, which in Heidi's case is as much a fallout of the narcissism associated with having it all as it is a fallout of her own—and Wasserstein's—idealism.

Heidi's alienation reaches a climax during her long speech, "Women, Where Are We Going," which according to Wasserstein is "probably the kernel of the play" (Rothstein 28). Characterized by David Patrick Stearns as a "nervous breakdown ... address on feminism" ("Lively, Liberated" 5D), it reflects Wasserstein's original inspiration for creating *The Heidi Chronicles*. "I wrote this play," she says, "because I had this image of a woman standing up at a women's meeting saying, 'I've never been so unhappy in my life,'" a feeling she acknowledges to have experienced "in me and in others" (Shapiro, "Chronicler" 90) and one that culminates for Heidi in a dramatic "cry of despair" (Weales 574).

The speech begins as a comic tour de force of what it means to be an "exemplary" and "exhausted" superwoman who does it all (229). Unprepared to give a formal speech, Heidi cites as her excuse a busy schedule from the previous day during which she taught classes, attended aerobics, picked up her children after school, prepared a gourmet meal, terminated an illicit affair, "finished writing ten pages of a new book," helped to feed the homeless, and "relieved any fears that [her banker husband] 'might' be getting old by 'doing it' in the kitchen" (229). The breathless spiel acts as a humorous treatment—or, more pointedly, as a satiric ridicule—of superwoman's impossible standards.

Midway through her speech, she begins to imagine the lives of seven women who attended a recent exercise class with her. In some respects, each one denotes an individual aspect of her superwoman model, but on the whole they seem to represent what Wasserstein presumably views as a cross-section of middle-class women: two young mothers "heatedly debating the [nursery school] reading program," one "woman [Heidi's] mother's age," one socialite with "perfect red nails," a "naked gray-haired woman extolling the virtues of brown rice and women's fiction," and "two twenty-seven-year-old hotshots" who "pulled out their alligator datebooks and began madly to call the office" (229–30).

Most likely, Heidi had long ago concluded how little she had in common with these women, but on this particular occasion she experiences an unbearable discomfort and alienation that snaps into the open when she drops the contents of her bag in the locker room.

Feeling both "worthless" and "superior" to these seven women, she
tells the Plaza Hotel audience, "I'm embarrassed—no, humiliated—
in front of every woman in that room. I'm envying women I don't
even know. I'm envying women I don't even like" (231). In short,
Heidi is acknowledging that she "is a woman alone" (Shapiro,
"Chronicler" 92). She "wants to be included in the group," says Joan
Allen, but she "can't find any peace or comfort in relating to any of
them" (Rothstein 28), and to make matters worse, she also suspects
that they do not like her. "I'm sure the mothers ... think women like
me chose the wrong road," says Heidi, that "it's a pity they made
such a mistake, that empty generation" (231).

The virtual absence of men in this speech highlights the fact
that they have less to do with Heidi's anguish than her sisters, and,
unfortunately, by the time Heidi delivers her talk, the women in the
locker room are merely bit players in the growing list of those who
have entered her life and left her blank. She has long ago lost con-
tact with the women from the rap group, and she cannot depend on
the mutual support and interest of Susan and her power-shower
counterparts. Abandoned, therefore, by their "settling-for or ... sell-
ing-out" (Leonard 70), Heidi feels saddened and "betrayed by her
contemporaries"—by their materialism, by their forsaken friendship,
and especially by the perception that they "have lost all touch with
feminist values"—and, as a result, she "has a meltdown" (Gerard,
review of *Heidi* 38): "I don't blame the ladies in the locker room for
how I feel. I don't blame any of us.... It's just that I feel stranded. And
I thought that the whole point was that we wouldn't feel stranded. I
I thought the point was that we were all in this together" (232).

According to Laurie Winer, Heidi's speech seems paradoxically
to suggest not only that she has "failed herself in some profound
way" but also that she feels "more blameful, than guilty" (C16). During a particularly reflective moment in *Bachelor Girls*, Wasserstein
writes that the "self-recrimination for not being a certain kind of
woman, a certain kind of mother, a certain kind of complete person is a quiet but constant undertow, a persistent dull ache" (148).
By feeling worthless beside the women in the locker room, Heidi
is largely internalizing her failures and thus experiencing the kind
of self-recrimination that Wasserstein herself has apparently

endured. Heidi, however, also senses that the ladies of the locker room do not approve of her, and when external forces—especially, other women—project their disapproval for not being that certain kind of woman or mother, Wasserstein, like Heidi, becomes understandably resentful: "Are they saying that women who decided to fulfill their potential have made a mistake? That's completely unfair," she says. "It makes you feel stranded. It makes you feel part of a tidal wave" (Rothstein 28).

In echoing Heidi's line about feeling stranded, Wasserstein not only names the play's crisis but also implies that the most blameful source of Heidi's alienation is disintegrated sisterhood. "If we were all in this together, why does it feel so separate now?". Feminism, she says, made options available to women that previous generations could not imagine. "But that's the personal pursuit. That is not the 'We' .... What's missing is the 'We'" (Rothstein 28).

For many, the problem of sisterhood, especially as Wasserstein presents it in this play, raises several questions. In "Feminism, Postmodernism, and *The Heidi Chronicles*," for instance, Bette Mandl writes that any dream of commonality and "the unitary picture of 'woman' it evokes, have been shown to resemble the totalizing patriarchal visions they hoped to displace" (121). Applied to Wasserstein, the "unitary picture" is the unifying spirit of sisterhood that she and Heidi not only idealize but expect others to practice, a position that Helene Keyssar deems "aggressively monologic" (97). As Kathleen P. Jones notes, the "kind of commitment that is expected from a sister exacts a toll that is not always consistent with the feminist stress on autonomy and self-development" (808). Expecting universal conformity to sisterhood may be a monolithic point of view, in which case Heidi—and Wasserstein—expect more from women than they have a right to expect.

A second issue involves Heidi herself. According to Laurie Winer, the "person who has let Heidi down is none other than Heidi herself." Although Winer believes that one "is not made unhappy by sticking close to her values in life, even as others fall by the wayside" (Laurie Winer C16), she also suggests that Heidi's "ungenerous trait of sitting in judgment" (C13) makes her no more reliable a "sister" than those who have failed to support her.

During her speech, for instance, Heidi makes it clear that she feels left out by the women in the locker room, but at the same time she also exhibits what Winer characterizes as a "need to condemn" (Laurie Winer C13). "I'm sure the woman with the son at Harvard is miserable to her daughter-in-law," says Heidi near the end of her speech. "I'm sure the gray-haired woman is having a bisexual relationship with a female dockworker and driving her husband crazy. I'm sure the hotshots have screwed a lot of thirty-five-year-old women, my classmates even, out of jobs, raises, and husbands" (231). In truth, she barely masks her condescension, which is especially evident during the women's discussion about the benefits of certain designer sneakers—not a terribly uncommon topic of conversation for an aerobics class but one Heidi finds so impossibly shallow that "at this point," she says, "I decided I would slip out and take my place in the back row of the class" (230).

According to Winer, rhetoric such as this, which Heidi also employs with more comic effects about the "blandish" Lisa Rosenbaum (202), "soon enough reveals [Heidi's] own bias" against women who are not like her (Laurie Winer C16), a point that impugns her own despair about feeling stranded. One might argue that Heidi's comments reflect her growing disillusionment with the increasingly gilded values she perceives in the women she knows, but in truth her remarks still intimate the kind of selective sisterhood Janie Blumberg evinces when Harriet announces her engagement and Janie seems not just unsupportive, but mean.

Even the uncontrollably jaded Susan also hints that Heidi is not always there for her. "Heidi will drop anything ... even a chance to see me," she says at consciousness-raising (181). Years later Susan likewise notes that with Heidi in London, she had to depend on others to smooth her transition to New York. Although Heidi's career rationally explains her absence in Susan's life at the time, Heidi is unable, it seems, to accept the similar demands of Susan's career not too long afterwards. In terms of female friendship, in other words, not only could Heidi probably act like a better friend herself, but there is also, finally, this to consider: the value of sisterhood notwithstanding, Heidi's best friend in this play is not Susan or any other woman. It is Peter Patrone.

The final issue—and the most controversial—is that many critics regard Heidi's disillusionment as evidence that *The Heidi Chronicles* stands as an "indictment of the failure of the women's movement" (Laurie Winer C16). According to John Beaufort, for
instance, although "Wasserstein dramatizes the ways in which Heidi
and her liberated sisters have made use of their newfound, hard-won
freedom," the play also demonstrates that Heidi's increasing isolation and sadness correlate directly with "the losses in idealism and
selfless dedication that have accompanied the gains of the women's
movement" ("Bright Facades" 24).

At the heart of this failure, says David Patrick Stearns, is that
the "feminist ideals of the 1960s fade[d] into the greed of the 80s"
and into a liberation that ultimately became "empty" when it abandoned its communal spirit for "self-glorification" ("Lively, Liberated"
5D). More specifically, says Beaufort, once they "triumphed in their
battles 'to be me,' the friends of the encounter sessions seem to have
forgotten the ideals they once cherished, and concentrated instead
on advancing their careers and realizing their personal ambitions"
("Bright Facades" 24). As an incurable idealist, however, Heidi committed herself to feminist ideals, and having lost the support she had
counted on, she tells Peter near the play's end that she does not "have
a life ... that works" for her (235). Rather than "an advocate of the
women's movement," then, she seems more like "one of its victims"
(Kramer 81).

Much to the chagrin of Lynda Hart and Peggy Phelan, both
Heidi and Wasserstein act, therefore, as "spokeswomen for a feminism that failed, that left women like Heidi 'stranded.'" With that
word, claim Hart and Phelan, Heidi answers her speech on
"Women, Where Are We Going" with "Nowhere," a conclusion
that they argue, however, indicts not feminism, but the limitations
of Wasserstein's "monolithic" feminist vision (2–3). Like Hart and
Phelan, Corinne Robins feels "horrified" and "angry" at Wasserstein and at the play's alleged imputation of the women's movement.
Stating that feminism "is presented as at best a quaint but somewhat dangerous aberration of the recent past," Robins denounces
the "betrayals of the Wendy Wassersteins ... who while profiting
from the movement have set out to undermine it" (4).

Wasserstein vehemently denies that *The Heidi Chronicles* represents any ultimate statement on feminism, let alone an indictment of it (Elder 29). "I don't look back on feminism with anger," she says with exasperation. "I'm a feminist.... I think the fight for equality isn't over" (Christy 10). According to Linda Winer, the play simply "dares to ask the hard questions" about the women's movement, an observation with which I agree ("Real People" 7). For example, although Heidi's inherent idealism to causes feminist and otherwise exacerbates the eventual isolation she never anticipated, her alienation is very profound and raw, almost too private for public reflection. But Deborah Rosenfelt and Judith Stacey point out that "denying the existence of a problem some have designated as the feminization of loneliness will only privatize the pain" (348), a condition Wasserstein rejects and bravely "dares" to explore through Heidi's speech.

*The Heidi Chronicles* also dares to probe the relationship of the women's movement to societal models of success and consumerism. To some extent, in fact, Wasserstein would agree with Robert Brustein's wry observation that she "seems to suggest that the feminist movement ... has succeeded largely in introducing women to the ravening competitiveness of the 80s ... [and in] adapting women to the worst qualities of men." Although to me this results more in a "subterranean assault" on the "yuppie standard" than an indictment of feminism ("Extremis" 34), Wasserstein "has a strong point to make about lost values" (McGuigan 77). In short, she dares to question the misguided opportunism that has overshadowed feminism's agenda of reform and female community.

"What distresses" Wasserstein, then, says Nina Burleigh, "is the way things have turned out, the way the old solidarity has collapsed into the new individualism" (8). However, as Paula Span notes, "neither Heidi nor Wasserstein would repudiate the movement" (G7). For certain, at the end of the play, when Scoop says to Heidi, "So I was right all along. You were a true believer," Heidi responds, "I don't see how it could be any other way" (247). Wasserstein devotedly remains a true believer, too, says Span (G7), while Heidi, concludes Brustein, "will no doubt continue to battle on behalf of her sex for equal rights and recognition" ("Extremis" 34).

Although Wasserstein clearly, then, does not renounce the women's movement, what continues to fuel this controversy and extend it well beyond the failure of sisterhood is the revelation in the last scene that Heidi has adopted a baby girl. According to Sharon Elder, some critics—among them, feminist critics—regard Heidi's "almost palpable happiness" in the last scene as the most blatant instance altogether of "Wasserstein's indictment of the movement. The message, they claim, is that if women had just stayed home in the first place to have babies, they wouldn't now be so frustrated, lonely, overwhelmed, and exhausted" (29). Although Elder, perhaps, distorts the gist of critical response to the message, hardly anyone, it seems, can justify Wasserstein's ending.

In the first place, as Bette Mandl legitimately argues, "Wasserstein has not ... prepared the audience for this unexpected turn of events" (125). Though Corinne Robins contends that the play's fertility discussions, multiple pregnancies, baby shower, and Peter's role as a pediatrician prove that the "subtext of *The Heidi Chronicles* ... is children" (4), these matters highlight the lives of other characters, not Heidi, and they especially offer no clue that she herself might consider adopting a child. Interestingly, as archival materials show, Wasserstein originally intended in the scene preceding the last one for Heidi to tell Peter that she wanted a child. Indecisive about how to proceed from there, Wasserstein shows in one scenario that Heidi asks Peter's help for an adoption (*Chronicles* notebook, box 3, folder 4) and, in another, that she considers talking "about children" to Fran, now a midwife living in Minnesota, where Heidi says she plans to teach at Carleton College (*Chronicles* ms., box 4, folder 8). Wasserstein deleted these adoption references, she says, because the "more important thread in Heidi's scene with Peter was that Stanley was ill," adding that "you also have to cut through time or the play drags" (personal interview 1995). By leaving out any suggestion whatsoever about adoption, though, it seems to many like an "unmotivated conclusion" (Matuz 218), one merely "tacked on" to bring the play to its conclusion (Kissel, "'Heidi' Grows Up" 35).

With little insight into or justification for Heidi's decision, therefore, critics have savaged the last scene not only for its unexpectedness but also for its implications. Sylviane Gold, for example, argues that with her adoption, Heidi's "sense of sadness and betrayal is assuaged by proxy, as it were" (A13). This perspective suggests that the baby is a "glib solution" (Simon, "Partial Autobiographies" 49), one aimed to provide for Heidi either "a cure for the mopes" (Leonard 70) or the impression of "selfless fulfillment" (Gussow, "Heffalump" C13). However, as Gerald Weales points out, "why single parenthood should fill the vacuum in her life is never clear in the script" (574), especially since the play contains only one unconvincing and vague statement from her about wanting a family (211).

According to Elder, having a child is "emphatically *not* Wasserstein's prescription for solving the mid-life blues of single career women" (29). "Heidi doesn't say that the baby is the answer," contends Wasserstein (Span G7). Heidi also does not say that "her generation was sacrificed to the women's movement and that female fulfillment must come through babies" (Hubbard 106). Heidi, insists Wasserstein, simply "makes a life for herself" (Span G7). "It's something that a lot of single women my age are doing" (personal interview 1995), she says, and though "very demanding," it also adds "so many dimensions" (Barney 54).

From a feminist standpoint, however, this position leads to another impasse. According to Nina Burleigh, several "prominent women—Betty Friedan and Helen Gurley Brown among them—have criticized the play's ending ... [as a] false solution to a false dilemma ... having to choose between a career and having a family" (Burleigh 1). The real dilemma, say many feminists, is that society, in continuing to regard women as its primary caretakers, still does little to ease the burden of choices that men, on the other hand, can make without forethought or recrimination. Friedan, in particular, says that she was disturbed by the ending because in "depicting Heidi as troubled over career and family, Wendy Wasserstein inadvertently fed a media hype, a new feminine mystique about the either/or choices in a woman's life" (Burleigh 1). Along these lines, Heidi's decision seems, in fact, like a hybrid of "having it all," one that simulates the prescription Lillian Cornwall makes to Harriet in *Isn't It Romantic* to have a child and pursue a career while dispensing with marriage.

To offset all the caviling that the play's conclusion seems on many levels like a "cop out" (Gold A13), I prefer to see Heidi's adoption mainly as a device, one that allows the perennially idealistic Heidi to envision the future. This approach materializes as Scoop asks her during the final scene if she is happy. "Well, I have a daughter," responds Heidi, "[and] there's a chance, just a millinotion, that Pierre Rosenbaum and Judy Holland will meet.... And he'll never tell her it's either/or, baby. And she'll never think she's worthless unless he lets her have it all. And maybe, just maybe, things will be a little better. And, yes, that does make me happy" (246–47).

As this short speech indicates, Heidi and her adoption—and the reasons for her adoption—are not the real focus of the play's conclusion. Judy is. As Bette Mandl muses, Heidi's "hope of a better future for Judy [could] be framed as a feminist vision of possibility" (126). Inextricably bound to her own experiences, Heidi's closing lines about either/or echo Scoop's ultimatum to her at the end of Act 1, and when she rejects it then as "simply not true," he tells her, "that's why you 'quality time' girls are going to be one generation of disappointed women" (202). In the future that Heidi imagines for her daughter, however, Scoop's son will never say these words to Judy. In the future that Heidi imagines, Judy will never think she is worthless unless Pierre lets her have it all, a declaration reminiscent of what she said in Ann Arbor nearly twenty years earlier about their daughters feeling worthwhile (182). Heidi wishes, in other words, for what narrowly missed her own lifetime: feminist idealism becoming society's reality, and a future in which Judy can fulfill her potential without recrimination and thus become, in Wasserstein's framework of mothers and daughters, a woman who is "(not) her mother."

Judy, then, represents—in Heidi's words—a "heroine for the twenty-first" century (248). In a play that examines the impact of the women's movement and dares to ask questions, Heidi's adoption says, perhaps, that "the next generation will make the connections" she did not (Richards, "Life and Loves" E6). In this way, the adoption is a fitting conclusion, one that not only gives credence to Heidi's lifelong commitment as a "true believer," but also places

Heidi's personal and political involvements in feminism in the context of the future and justifies the ongoing work of the women's movement despite failure or setbacks.

The play ends with a "slide of Heidi triumphantly holding Judy in front of a museum banner for a Georgia O'Keefe [sic] retrospective" (249), an exhibit that did in fact take place at New York's Metropolitan Museum of Art in 1988–1989. On one level, this last display represents a professional triumph and grand finale for Heidi. In the dramatic world, it suggests that Heidi herself, after years of crusading for the need to highlight the achievements of women artists, has finally succeeded in doing so. On another level, however, an image of women past, present, and future emerges. If, as Wasserstein says, *The Heidi Chronicles* represents "a play of ideas" (Shapiro, "Chronicler" 92), the last idea conveyed by this image is not an indictment of feminism or of its leaky solidarity but on the contrary a celebration of its unfinished work and its intergenerational alliances.

# 5

# Of Life and Men

Tessie, as your Aunt Pfeni can tell you, a good man is hard to find.
—Gorgeous Teitelbaum in *The Sisters Rosensweig*

I didn't have a "you" in my life at sixteen.
I'm certainly not going to have a "you" in my life now.
—Sara Goode to Merv Kant in *The Sisters Rosensweig*

It's either/or.
—Scoop Rosenbaum to Heidi Holland in *The Heidi Chronicles*

On many levels, *The Sisters Rosensweig* represents a departure for Wasserstein. Tightening her time frame to a single weekend, she abandons her trademark episodic style for a more traditionally unified structure, and though she continues to examine the profound effects of the women's movement on private life, she nonetheless renders its overt politics and rhetoric to subtle suggestion. Of all the differences, however, the most significant involves character development: her uncommon women—formerly college students, college graduates, and thirtysomethings—have reached the heretofore uncharted passage of middle age.

It "was important to me to write a play about three uncommon women who are not 23," says Wasserstein (Miller H1). "The fact of the matter is: three middle-aged women on a stage who are accomplished and successful and not caricatures in our culture is still a surprise…. And that's why I wanted to write this play" (Miller H8). Although Alison Lurie pursued a similar mission with her 1984 Pulitzer Prize novel *Foreign Affairs*, few writers have ventured into the scantily examined territory of women's life after forty, and when they have, notes Paul Hodgins, the characters "are frequently

ghettoized ... [and] sketchily drawn as harridans, mindless dither-
ers, nags or dangerously unbalanced Medeas" (Hodgins, "Southern
California" 8).

In Wasserstein's play, the three Rosensweig sisters are portrayed instead as thoughtful, middle-aged women who have reached
crossroads in their lives. Like their counterparts in *The Three Sisters*, which Wasserstein says she loosely imitates, the Rosensweigs
"need to find Chekhov's Moscow of the spirit, to find their place in
the world" (Barnes, "Wendy's Wonderful" 24), and though they
share with her earlier heroines a concern about their present and
future, they are by virtue of their more mature years the first to
begin seriously "asking themselves significant questions about their
past" (Richards, "School of Life" H5). As Lee Barney notes, in "her
own way, each sister in the play struggles with identity crises, trying to rationalize the choices she has made in her life" (51). The
result is a middle-aged vision with a feminist slant, and though it
links a number of identity issues "about being American, Jewish, and
woman" (Wasserstein, Free Library 1995), the play pointedly raises
the question as well of how uncommon women make room in their
uncommon lives for loving, sustained relationships with men.

Although critics have analyzed the Jewish element most extensively, it acts more for me as a sparring partner, so to speak, for
Wasserstein's retrospective and feminist objectives, especially as it
affects the relationship between past and present in the life of the
eldest sister, Sara Goode. Like Wasserstein, the Rosensweigs grew
up in a traditional Jewish family in Brooklyn (Burleigh 8), but for
reasons never made quite clear in the play, Sara views her background as a symptom of Old World values or as a liability to her
international business affairs, and, consequently, she "aggressively
nullifies her New York Jewish upbringing" (Stuart 63). In fact, says
Lee Barney, "with her fake British accent, chintz-filled house and
snobby beau, [she] has done everything short of converting to repudiate her Jewish roots in Brooklyn" (51).

Sara's "WASP Disneyland" in London becomes disrupted with
the arrival of sister Gorgeous Teitelbaum, who "much to Sara's hor-
ror ... wears her Brooklyn-Jewish roots on her frilly pink sleeves"
(Stuart 77). As "the only halfway devout Jew" of the Rosensweigs

(Watt, "Drawing-Room" 77), Gorgeous induces Sara's quick ire during the first act when shortly before the arrival of dinner guests she insists on some semblance of Sabbath observance by lighting candles and reciting a brief prayer. A quintessential yenta (Kissel, "Sharpened 'Sisters'" 74) to whom "'sisterhood is powerful' suggests Hadassah" (Linda Winer, "Sisters" 76), Gorgeous represents everything Sara has rejected.

On her own, Gorgeous has neither the resources nor the acumen to force Sara's showdown with their Jewish past. However, as Jan Stuart observes, Gorgeous' "in-your-face ethnicity is multiplied by the arrival of Mervyn Kant" (77), a faux furrier who is traveling in Europe with the American Jewish Congress and who "sifts all discourse through his Jewish identity" (Linda Winer, "Sisters" 76). Because, as Sara notes, he "always come[s] back" to his roots (54), she thinks not only that Merv has a "narrow perspective" (53) but also that he judges her as someone who has "assimilated beyond her wildest dreams, and now ... wants to come home," an assumption she denies (57).

Although the question of Jewish identity creates considerable tension between Merv and Sara, it quickly metamorphoses into sexual tension. After "a somewhat quick quickie" on the night they meet (Watt, "Drawing-Room" 77), Sara the next day rebuffs any possibility of a future together. Not only does she find Merv's Jewish world "very different" from hers, but she also scoffs at his attempt to become her "knight in shining armor" (81). "I didn't have a 'you' in my life at sixteen," she says. "I'm certainly not going to have a 'you' in my life now" (82). For me, this exchange clearly illustrates that, as Sara's foil, Merv turns the play's Jewish factor into a sparring partner for its feminist factor, because despite his formidable Jewish rhetoric and identity, Merv's presence in the play ultimately contributes more to its reflections about Sara's relationships with men.

By the end of the play, the conflict generated by the Jewish element acting on the feminist one concludes with a cease-fire on both counts. Once she realizes that "however hard she has worked, Jewish identity is not discardable," Sara comes to terms somewhat with her past and abandons the hard-line assimilation by lovingly reciting "her given name, the ever-so-Jewish Rosensweig" (Kissel, "Sharpened

'Sisters'" 74). At the same time, Sara also admits—grudgingly—that
she likes the "sweet, loudmouthed furrier" after all (Kirkpatrick
A11). Nonetheless, she tells him, "I don't think about us getting
married, and I don't even need to get our children together" (105).
Consequently, as these lines reveal, the cease-fire, however warm
and affectionate, has a hedging tone. It not only says that Sara rel-
ishes her independence, but it also suggests, however faintly, a
residue from troubled relationships in her past, an impasse that represents for me an underlying shadow that Wasserstein wants to cast
over this play.

   Although Sara's relationship with Merv epitomizes Wasserstein's use of Jewish culture as an accessory to her feminist objectives, she integrates the two in other ways as well. While working
on *The Heidi Chronicles*, Wasserstein says she "deliberately didn't
write Heidi as Jewish because of what happened to me in *Miami*"
(personal interview 1995). An "autobiographical musical comedy
[that] never got beyond a workshop production in 1986" (Miller
H8), *Miami* followed Wasserstein's other "Jewish" play, *Isn't It
Romantic*, and folded in part, she says, because "they said it was too
Jewish." In fact, because "it's about women, it's comedy, and it's
Jewish," Wasserstein believes that critics and producers alike treat
her work sometimes with a "triple whammy" (personal interview
1995). "Nobody in Hollywood says, oh, boy—let's do a play about
a 54-year-old woman … who still has possibilities," let alone one
whose last name is Rosensweig (Miller H8). It seems, therefore, that
she deliberately showcases all three in *The Sisters Rosensweig*, merging the Jewish component with a feminist one, and—à la fem-
en(act)ment—gives both the play itself and the act of writing it a
political agenda.

   In addition to these motivations, Wasserstein at the same time
wanted the play "deliberately set on the eve of a momentous historical event" (*Rosensweig* ix), specifically that "August weekend of
1991 when the Soviet Union was teetering on the revolution that was
to turn it back into Russia" (Barnes, "Sisters" 72). As *The Heidi
Chronicles* demonstrates, setting plays within historic frameworks is
one of Wasserstein's cyclic passions. "In a way," she says, "what I do
is a lot like British theatre. It's a large canvas in which you see the

social and historical change, and then the personal change, and how they reflect in each other" (Stone 2).

For *The Sisters Rosensweig*, setting the play expressly during the break-up of the Soviet Union provides both a creative and logical rationale to her would-be detractors for its being "steeped in Jewish culture" (Gussow, "Comedy" C3). As Clive Barnes explains, the dismantling of the Russian republic created an atmosphere in real and stage life "for ethnic reassessment. Certainly a time to think about anti–Semitism and what it has meant to the makeup of the world still at large" ("Wendy's Wonderful" 24). In this vein, Tessie Goode's school project about her mother's past, her short-lived intention to join the Lithuanian resistance with her "dimwitted boyfriend" Tom Valiunus (Richards, "School of Life" H6), and her desire to know more about the roots of her ethnic identity have a historical frame of reference, one that also accounts for Sara's own reflections and justifies Merv's "acutely sensitized radar for anti–Semitism" (Stuart 77).

Although the dissolution of the Soviet Union has a clear relationship to Jewish identity, it stands more for me as an inventive way to link Jewish politics with feminist intent. For one, the Soviet disintegration intensifies the focus on what it means to feel uncertain and unsettled. As Phoebe Hoban points out, "the sisters Rosensweig are in search of themselves, trying to find a sense of centeredness in a world that is out of control" (34). To emphasize the milieu of chaos further, therefore, Wasserstein's sociopolitical repertoire not only includes anti–Semitism but also skirts the edges of "AIDS, bisexuality, teenage rebellion," economic recession, and unemployment (Greene 33). In other words, the disintegration and bifurcation of social institutions complement the play's true nucleus: the personal disintegration and renewal of Sara, Gorgeous, and Pfeni, the core of which contains an inseparable, feminist disposition.

In retrospect, therefore, Sara's final words to Merv—suggesting romance, but forbidding commitment—reflect this disposition. When she declares her infatuation with him during their last scene together, says Howard Stein, she makes "her position clear: I don't want you to be the answer for me. And she means it" (25). Burned twice by failed marriages, Sara has learned, I suspect, that, despite her down mood right now, an emotional commitment to Merv will not work. This conclusion merely reinforces what Wasserstein has quietly been tracking: specifically, that at the heart of the play's individual crises and feminist dialectic lies the uneasy relationship between a woman's career and her private life.

Tracing their lineage to *Uncommon Women and Others*, so to speak, the three uncommon sisters represent a "provocative slide rule of identity in today's achievement arena" (Kraft B7). As the brilliant managing director of the Hong Kong/Shanghai Bank, Sara has appeared "on the cover of *Fortune* twice" (10). Pfeni, a travel columnist, has previously published international, Margaret Mead–like studies of women and culture, and Gorgeous awaits a cable-television deal for her Boston radio show. However, says Lee Barney, despite "their apparent success, the sisters in Wasserstein's play seem painfully lonely" (50) or, at the very least, filled with what Wasserstein calls yearning and melancholy (Grossberg D1).

Although Gorgeous seems less troubled than her sisters until she reveals a few secrets at the close, Sara and Pfeni are noticeably "roiling with discontent" (Stuart 63). Sara describes herself at the onset, for instance, as a lonely and bitter woman (12), who, according to her daughter, has "desperate need of hope and rebirth" (7). Pfeni, on the other hand, seems inexplicably unable to leave her somewhat unsatisfying job despite being "full of restless yearnings" to trek to Tajikistan and finish a book on gender and class (Kissel, "Family Circus" 47).

As "compulsive achievers" (Henry, "Reborn" 69), Sara and Pfeni illustrate how well-educated women have become enormously successful beneficiaries of the liberal feminist agenda to make myriad careers available to women. Yet, because they seem "vaguely maladjusted" (Richards, "School of Life" H5), critics have accused Wasserstein—again—of indicting the women's movement or of having used her heroines' unhappiness as a vehicle to indict the movement themselves. "Options flourish," says Howard Stein, for instance. "But in the final analysis, they offer neither solace nor refuge for the condition that life is wanting" (22).

Agreeing with Stein's assessment, David Patrick Stearns says that Wasserstein has undoubtedly "upset her feminist supporters" with this play, especially since the "two who have pursued glamorous careers ... realize they're neurotic, lonely and painfully estranged" ("Sisters" 4D). In this vein, according to Linda Winer, *The Sisters Rosensweig* hardly seems like "the direction some of us desired for the woman who broke mainstream barriers with *The Heidi Chronicles*" ("Sisters" 76). To complicate matters, critics also conclude that Wasserstein has apparently agreed that "it's all worthless if she ain't got a good husband to come home to—as, we ultimately learn, none of the Rosensweig girls has" (Feingold, review of *Sisters* 84).

Although this conclusion illustrates an astonishingly hasty and inaccurate rush to judgment by the critics, it is not difficult to see why a less-informed audience might leave *The Sisters Rosensweig* with this impression. On the surface, all three of them seem to act at times as though the absence of men—or of reliable men—in their lives lies at the root of whatever discontent each experiences in the play. "I miss sex. I always liked sex," Sara tells Merv (58), and though she erects a few barriers around the expected continuation of their relationship, the fact remains that it takes a mere 48 hours to become smitten with him. At the same time, apparently for the convenience of male companionship, she dates Nicholas Pym, a "pompous English prig" she does not particularly like (Barnes, "Wendy's Wonderful" 24). His longtime presence in Sara's life makes her self-characterized loneliness particularly convincing, in fact, since he proves himself not only an incredible bore but also, according to Tessie, a "socially acceptable, racist, sexist" male who wines and dines sixteen-year-old models on the sly (10), all of which provokes Gorgeous to name him "a philanderer and a Nazi" (34).

In the meantime, the never-married Pfeni has for the last three years engaged in an insecure relationship with an "internationally renowned director and bisexual" (17), Geoffrey Duncan, who she steadily worries might someday leave her—as he eventually does—because he misses men. Before he departs, however, she seems clearly willing during the second act to end her fabulous career for him, declaring "I'm not going to travel anymore. I want to stay with you" (69); and when he does exit her life, she—momentarily, at least—falls apart.

Gorgeous, the only married one of the three, reveals that her husband's firm has dissolved its partnership, leaving him unemployed as a lawyer for the past two years. Henry is not "even looking for a job," she says, but worse than that, he "dresses up in a trench coat and goes out to prowl around the bars" in hopes of becoming the next Raymond Chandler or Dashiell Hammett (93). The deleterious effect of Henry's mid-life crisis on their financial affairs—and, so Gorgeous hints, on their sex life together—does not, however, deter Gorgeous from playing matchmaker for the other two.

Within seconds after meeting Merv Kant, who does not find Sara very "'funsy'" at first, Gorgeous says, "Maybe you should marry her." When he notes, "I've only spent five minutes with her," Gorgeous responds, "So what? Some people know at first sight" (28). As for Pfeni, Gorgeous believes that her younger sister is simply wasting her time with Geoffrey. "Don't you think it's time she considered someone even remotely available?" she asks Sara. "Don't you think it's time she stopped living her life like she was on an extended junior year abroad?" (33). Convinced that Pfeni is wandering herself "right out of the marketplace," Gorgeous asks, "don't you want what any normal woman wants?" (72).

In response to Gorgeous' remarks, Michael Feingold wryly imagines the prospect of "a postperformance discussion, Camille Paglia and Susan Faludi mud wrestling over the dubious assumptions that question implies." In her previous plays, he says, Wasserstein "pulled these hearth-and-home sentiments into a troubled, ironic dialectic with much different views" (review of *Sisters* 84). Gorgeous, however, is not Wasserstein, and despite how critics and audiences regard the Rosensweigs' trysts, to think the playwright asserts that "a girl—even an updated independent 90s sort of girl—is happier when she has a nice man" oversimplifies Wasserstein's task in this play (Linda Winer, "Sisters" 76).

Even Feingold knows this represents "neither a sensible nor an accurate summation of the state of intelligent women in the 1990s. Nor, more to the point, does it sum up the dynamic activity Wasserstein's play has been graphing" (review of *Sisters* 84). Though audiences might conclude that without a loving husband "the sisters' achievements are worldly and hollow," he says, "I don't think people who publish books and make financial megadeals view their work that way" (84).

I do not think Sara and Pfeni view it that way, either, and though men do play a pivotal role in their lives and in this play, the dynamic activity Wasserstein has been graphing should not lead, as Jack Kroll presupposes, to the deduction that a "feminist writer" finally wants to show her female characters as being "saved by a real *mensch*" who will cheer away the blues wrought by their single-mindedly pursuing career fulfillment ("Gotta Have Heart" 104). On the contrary, in fact, the sisters Rosensweig prove quite convincingly that they do not *need* men. As Paul Hodgins notes, they "have learned (or are in the painful process of learning) how to negotiate life's tortuous road map without a man. And each, in her own inimitable and often hilarious way, succeeds, although ... complete happiness remains a distant and possibly unattainable goal" ("Southern California" 8).

Though they do not need men to feel complete, the sisters Rosensweig like men, however, and remain open to being and falling in love. Sexual politics aside, most women feel the same, and any "feminism that fails to recognize these facts will, of necessity, fail" (Tong 24). Wasserstein clearly knows this; yet, as Jan Stuart says to pinpoint the problem, the sisters Rosensweig are—like Wasserstein's other uncommon women—"exceptionally intelligent, dauntingly overachieving and resultingly bereft of men capable of giving them what they need" (63).

Sandra Meyer, Wasserstein's older sister and the model for Lillian Cornwall in *Isn't It Romantic*, is in this play the inspiration for Sara Goode. Aptly described by Walter Shapiro as "one of the first generation of pioneering executive women" ("Chronicler" 92), she is credited, for instance, with being the "marketing executive for General Foods, [who] came up with the idea of putting Tang on the moon" (Barney 50). Before she died in December 1997 from breast cancer, Meyer compiled a resume that reads like a dream-list for women's business studies: "first female product-group manager at General Foods, in 1969; the first female president of a division of American Express, in 1980; and the first female to run corporate affairs as a senior officer at Citicorp, in 1989." Remembering her from childhood as a "mythical, glamorous alternative to the bouffant-hair-sprayed mothers at the Parent-Teacher Association," Wasserstein says Meyer "was always the only woman along her corridor [at General Foods] who wasn't sitting outside an office glued behind a typewriter and a telephone" ("Don't Tell Mother" 196).

Musing on her sister's career, however, Wasserstein said in 1996, "I wish that my sister would tell me what toll her life has taken on her.... My sister would say that life takes its toll, male or female, period. I heartily disagree. I can't help but wonder what difference it would have made in my sister's personal or corporate life if she had been a man" ("Don't Tell Mother" 197). Because *The Sisters Rosensweig* is, as Linda Winer states, "Sara's story at heart" ("Sisters" 76), Wasserstein, I believe, imagines the toll somewhat through the private life of Sara, who is an unmarried career mother and double divorcee, as Meyer was.

Meyer, to whom Wasserstein dedicates *The Sisters Rosensweig*, distanced herself from the toll on Sara, however, saying that her issues were "different" in both her private and political realm (Miller H8). "Sandra would say that if you're a player, gender shouldn't be an issue. But, for my generation, gender *is* the issue." What her sister would not discuss, says Wasserstein to exemplify the point, "is why so many of her male corporate contemporaries have become chairmen and she did not" ("Don't Tell Mother" 197, 199). Wasserstein does not address the glass ceiling in Sara Goode's career—if, in fact, one exists for Sara—but in the general arena of gender issues and as an undercurrent to the play's middle-aged retrospective, Wasserstein casually encircles her heroines' love affairs with a subtle suggestion about the interplay of career and private life, and— evincing a materialist mode—she observes, though never resolves, the seeming inevitability that women in high-octane careers have "confused relationships with men" (Hoban 34).

To appreciate Wasserstein's position on the interaction of the two, as well as the understated way she observes it, one must first discard the misconception that manlessness or, in Gorgeous' case, man-listlessness has caused the sense of "pain ... anger ... and simple sadness" the sisters Rosensweig exude in the play (Richards, "School of Life" H5). Their vulnerability, so palpable at times, sits instead at the thick of their middle-aged self-analysis, which—as Wasserstein reveals—involves much more than man trouble.

Although each has her own crosses to bear, they share one sorrow in common: the recent death of their mother, Rita Rosensweig, who pervades their thoughts, conversation, and—given the circumstances—their understandably brittle emotions. In fact, as Gorgeous notes to Merv, their mother's passing explains in part "why we're all here for [Sara's] birthday" (31). In Sara's case, particularly, Rita Rosensweig's demise involves a number of issues. For one, because of a recent hysterectomy, she did not attend the funeral. Sara's hysterectomy alone could explain her brittleness and fatigue, but, more importantly, it *does* explain why at 54 she not only seems depressed "about aging" (Barney 51), but also might begin to mourn the alleged loss of her appeal as a woman. If so, she does not feel "sexually repressed" or hungry for a man in her life, as Doug Watt claims ("Drawing-Room" 77), but anxious to reestablish her sexual being for her own self-image, a point that sensibly accounts for her "reluctant attraction" to (Brustein, "The Editorial Play" 34) and willingness to sleep with the Jewish nationalist and "odd man in," Merv Kant (Watt, "Sister" 77).

Although Gorgeous says that their mother "really missed saying good-bye" to her, Sara does not appear to feel guilty about missing the funeral. Gorgeous' comment seems to imply, instead, that Sara's absence owed less to the hysterectomy than to past conflicts between Sara and their mother. When Gorgeous says Rita "wanted to see us all happy," Sara retorts, "We are happy, Gorgeous. It's just not our mother's kind of happiness" (36).

Returning to her recurring mother-daughter motif, Wasserstein, in this case, demonstrates how matriarchal influence still troubles Sara's life. Borrowing Lola Wasserstein's nickname for Sandra Meyer (Finn 366), Rita, recalls Gorgeous, referred to Sara as a brilliant "shtarker," which Pfeni defines as a "person who takes charge" or a "general in the Cossack army" (95). "I remember coming home with a 99," recollects Sara, "and her shrieking at me, 'Where's the other point?'" Adding wryly that she became a banker because "no one ever called me Gorgeous," Sara implies that she has been mulling the source and price of her past choices (36).

In addition to the hysterectomy and Rita's death, as well as all the emotional baggage accompanying both, Sara also worries about Tessie, her "near-radicalized daughter" (Watt, "Drawing-Room" 77), who threatens not only to abandon an Oxford education but also to join the Lithuanian resistance with her "dopey but good-natured punker boyfriend" (Simon, "The Best So Far" 100). "She's determined to make her life the opposite of mine," wails Sara. When Pfeni reminds her that this is "exactly what we set out to do because of our mother," Sara responds, "but we were right" (11). Despite her facetious remark, Tessie's rebellion concerns Sara and not only complicates her multifaceted mid-life retrospective but also provides another reason for her feeling "morally and spiritually adrift" (Richards, "School of Life" H5) and placing "her emotional life … in a … safe-deposit box" (Kroll, "Gotta Have Heart" 104).

Because of Rita's "strong influence on her adult daughters" (Gussow, "Comedy" C3), Pfeni also seems to be coping with the fallout of her mother's death. Pfeni's grief explodes when Geoffrey leaves, leading her to cry to Sara, "I don't want to lose Geoffrey and Mommy at the same time" (90). Complicating her remorse, though, she, like Sara, apparently has some unsettled history with their mother. When she remarks to Gorgeous, "I'm not every mother's dream daughter," Gorgeous tells her not to "waste [her] time rebelling against Mother anymore. She's not even here to enjoy it" (72).

Rita Rosensweig's death is not, however, the main thing making Pfeni restless, cranky, and "not at home in the world" (Stein 22). Tessie tells her that, according to Sara, "you compulsively travel because you have a fear of commitment, and when you do stay in one place, you become emotional and defensive" (7). Although, as critics suggest, this seems to imply that Pfeni, a "funky, peripatetic journalist" (Hoban 32), "restlessly ricochets between the world's flash points" (Kroll, "Gotta Have Heart" 104) and "lives more for the escape of travel than for the art of writing" (Henry, "Reborn" 69), she likes the lifestyle, has earned enormous respect for her work, and, as Sara knows, has "a true calling" for what she does (78).

Nevertheless, as Pfeni says at the outset, her "life is stuck" (17). On the edge of her own middle-aged retrospect, she not only has considered settling down with Geoffrey but also has begun to bring to terms her past journalistic life with the present one. As her *Life in the Afghan Village* illustrates, Pfeni formerly worked as a "journalistic voice of the oppressed masses" (Kissel, "Family Circus" 47), but after inexplicably abandoning the "political bent" of her work (Barnes, "Wendy's Wonderful" 24), she has now become "dissatisfied writing superficial travel articles" (Barney 50).

Pfeni's principal crisis in this play, as well as the main source of her unhappiness, then, centers on her career and, more specifically, on the fact that she "avoids the serious writing she should be doing" (Richards, "School of Life" H5). She tells Geoffrey that she has a "new book about gender and class working in a crock pot somewhere in Tajikistan" (68) and tells Sara that she needs "the hardship of the Afghan women and the Kurdish suffering to fill up my life for me" (77). As Judith Miller explains, unlike Sara, Pfeni "is passionate about her work, about her writing, but she seems to have trouble doing it. To escape finishing her long-in-progress book on women in Tajikistan, she travels endlessly, penning articles on 'Bombay by Night,' or 'Bombay by Day'" (H8).

As "the author's stand-in" (Gerard, 1992 review 70), Pfeni represents Wasserstein's own periodic writer's block. As Wasserstein herself explains, "I guess I was doing the same thing.... Like Pfeni, I was beginning to do too many essays, too much speaking, too many things other than writing plays." Calling it an "evasion—a way of putting off the confrontation with the blank first page," Wasserstein says that "Pfeni's not writing ... may be why this play was written" (Miller H8).

Unlike Wasserstein, however, Pfeni does not seem to recognize the syndrome. Reflecting on what she has told Sara she needs, Pfeni says that "if I'm that empty, then I might as well continue to wander to the best hotels, restaurants, and poori stands" (77). However, as Sara says of the Afghan and Kurdish women Pfeni misses, "how are you helping them if you don't tell their stories? Is it morally better to dispatch four-star Karachi hotel reviews? ... I think you care too much and you're looking for excuses not to" (77–8).

In this light, Geoffrey appears to have arrived at just the right time in Pfeni's life to provide the distraction she needed to justify changing or ending her stalled career. An "ebullient but labile

heterosexual" (Simon, "The Best So Far" 100), he charms everyone
"with high spirits and bitchy anecdotes," and together they seem like
a couple sincerely fond of each other (Oliver, "Chez Rosensweig"
105). Unfortunately, however, they can only squeeze their relationship in between his always being in rehearsal and her being "in
Timbuktu half the year" (17), and, ultimately, he understands before
she does that their careers matter to them as much as love does. "Of
course, we must cherish those that we love," he tells her. "But just
as important, people like you and me have to work even harder to
create the best art ... that we possibly can. And the rest, the children, the country kitchen, the domestic bliss, we leave to others who
will have different regrets" (69).

Although Pfeni initially feels very hurt when Geoffrey deserts
her, she rebounds quickly. If his leaving really mattered, says Alexis
Greene, she would suffer "for at least a week" (33), but it simply
makes her confront why she loved him in the first place and what
she really wants in her life. As she says to Gorgeous in her last
scene, "if you only write 'Bombay by Night' and you make sure to
fall in love with men who can never really love you back, one morning you wake up at forty in your big sister's house, and where you
should be seems sort of clear" (100–01).

Unlike her sisters, Gorgeous is "an ostensibly happily married
mother of four" (Miller H1) who "has wholeheartedly embraced
their late mother's dream" (Stuart 77) by adopting "attitudes that
belong to women raised 20 years before her" (Linda Winer, "Sisters" 76). As such, she acts as a foil to Sara, not only by parading
their Jewish past but also by interfering in Sara's domestic affairs
until, sternly rebuking her, Sara reminds Gorgeous, "you are not our
mother" (75).

Because she seems like a "ditzy, motor-mouthed Jewish matron"
(Barney 49), Gorgeous is a "virtual compendium of laugh-getting
quirks" and "apologetic materialism" (Richards, "School of Life" H5).
Loosely based on Wasserstein's other sister, Georgette Levis, Gorgeous outwardly lives up to her nickname, the same one Morris
Wasserstein gave to Levis, because, as Sandra Meyer noted, at "eight,
she was already elegant" (Saline 90). However, Gorgeous, a "bargain-
basement shopper" who "wears counterfeit couture" (Kron V12),

looks more "like a dish of raspberry sherbet wearing gold jewelry" who swoops into the play to accessorize her sisters' lives with men and fashion hints (Richards, "School of Life" H5). Although she has a career as a self-credentialed psychiatrist who dispenses advice like a "non–Teutonic Dr. Ruth" (Kroll, "Gotta Have Heart" 104), Gorgeous nonetheless strikes everyone as a "sublimely ridiculous housewife and radio personality" (Hoban 32).

Gorgeous knows the impression she conveys, and because she feels acutely left behind in the luster of her sisters' enormously successful and challenging careers, she has decided at mid-life to prove to herself and to others that she's not just an "upside-down-cake-of-a-Jewish-princess" (Kraft B7). This, for me, explains her restlessness and vulnerability in the play better than her husband's setbacks. Resenting general perception of her as a "superficial, unsophisticated suburban ... retro specimen" (Stearns, "Sisters" 4D), she tells Merv that The Dr. Gorgeous Show has made her a "real middle-aged success story" (31), and, on the basis of that achievement and her allegedly successful marriage, she accuses her sisters of jealousy. "Well, you can speak with your la-di-dah British accent," she screams at Sara, "and Pfeni can send my children postcards from every ca-ca-mamie capital in the world, but I know that deep inside both of you wish you were me" (75).

Because Gorgeous does not really believe this, she hopes a cable deal for her radio show will bring her the respectability she craves from others at this juncture in her life. It will not, but with or without the deal, she ends up proving to be a "special blend of philosopher and fool" anyway (Simon, "The Best So Far" 100). For instance, as the play eventually reveals, Gorgeous "stifles the constant stress of maintaining a cheery, or in her own word 'funsy' demeanor, when life is falling apart at home" (Vellela 13). Alluding to Henry's setbacks, Madeline Kahn, who won a Tony award for her portrayal of Gorgeous, admires the "way [Gorgeous] carries that burden, the way it is revealed and what it takes to reveal it" (Specter C9). In other words, Gorgeous discovers in this play that she possesses strengths unnoticed by everyone—herself included— and that, although her media career offers "just a little sparkle" (30), it will not bring her Sara's and Pfeni's spotlight and does not need to.

"Gorgeous is interesting in terms of feminism," says Wasserstein. "Her type is the easy butt of jokes. But in the end, I make her a person of dignity" (personal interview 1995). As Jan Stuart notes, Wasserstein does this by ultimately making Gorgeous an "alluringly paradoxical" figure who "subverts her own cliché status" by denying herself "her biggest pleasure when it arrives: a real-label outfit" (77). For all her alleged superficiality, Gorgeous knows that, with her husband's misfortune, "somebody's got to pay for [her children's] tuition this fall, and better Chanel than Henry or me" (103).

Gorgeous is also interesting in terms of feminism because, of all the Rosensweigs, she ostensibly is the only one who has it all. As Merv says, "So you're the sister who did everything right. You married the attorney, you had the children, you moved to the suburbs." Protesting, she says, "I am much more than that.... I am one of the first real jugglers" (30). Because she strikes no one as an uncommon woman, especially in comparison to her sisters, Gorgeous does not seem like a juggler. But she is. In fact, with four children and an unemployed, would-be sleuth and writer for a husband, Gorgeous provides both financial and domestic security for her family.

Like Sara and Pfeni, Gorgeous, despite having it all, ultimately reflects the toll Wasserstein observes regarding the interplay of career and private life for uncommon women. It is simply this: whatever the reasons, Wasserstein's uncommon woman seemingly and frequently cannot sustain satisfying relationships with men. At 40, Pfeni has never married and has discovered the impossibility of commitment with Geoffrey. Sara has divorced two husbands and "doubt[s] there will be a third" (27), and though Gorgeous' problems with Henry admittedly materialize from his unexpected unemployment, one has to wonder why he did not accompany her on this trip to London. Although Mel Gussow suspects that "each has difficulty with men" because they "seldom seem worthy of the Rosensweigs" (Gussow, "Comedy" C3), Wasserstein appears to suggest that in Sara's and Pfeni's situations, especially, men have difficulty with each of them and seldom seem willing to adjust.

If the exploration into the source of this toll seems muted, it is because in her persistent re-view of the toll, Wasserstein has already unveiled the causes. In *Uncommon Women and Others*, Kate Quin linked this toll to the way men perceived her extraordinary talent. "I guess it never occurred to me in college," she says, "that someone wouldn't want me to be quite so uncommon" (69). In *Isn't It Romantic*, Lillian Cornwall, predecessor to Sara Goode as a divorced mother and exceptional businesswoman, thought the toll was exacted by always having to be the one "to leave the office when the kid bumps his head on a radiator or slips on a milk carton.... I had a promising career, a child, and a husband," she tells her daughter, Harriet, and if "you're very conscientious, you still have to choose your priorities," which in Lillian's—and Sara's—case, meant choosing motherhood and career excellence over the demands of an unsupportive husband (134).

Janie Blumberg suffered the toll because of an ultimatum, the same one Scoop Rosenbaum eventually offered to Heidi: "It's either/or," he told her: either homemaker and part-time careerist, or full-time careerist and no Marty, no Scoop (202). For Heidi, the alter ego to Pfeni as a single career woman, the toll proceeded from her wanting the same things as Scoop: "Self-fulfillment. Self-determination. Self-exaggeration," in which case, he informed Heidi, "you'd be competing with me" (201).

As the plays reveal, then, the sources of the toll range in Wasserstein's eyes from the inability of men to understand the intellectual, professional, and career aspirations of the women who love them to an unwillingness by men to view the relationship as a supportive partnership. In *The Sisters Rosensweig*, Wasserstein effectively brings the toll to middle age, and though she manifests it by juxtaposing the sisters' careers alongside their past and present love life, the play neither traces nor resolves the causes but only observes the toll itself, albeit with a most subtle lens.

When asked why her uncommon women seemingly have few successful relationships with men, Wasserstein said, "it's about yearning"—about wanting fulfillment in many things and not wanting to make the compromises that men under the same circumstances can largely ignore (personal interview 1995). According to a 1995 study by Catalyst, a women's professional support organization founded in 1960 by Felice Schwartz, women executives from

Fortune 1000 companies reported workdays beginning at 4 A.M. before children awake and a need, therefore, for "sophisticated time-management skills, above-average physical stamina and supportive husbands—if they are married—to get ahead." In addition, revealed one senior vice-president and chief financial officer, women "face the daunting challenge of a 'white noise' of male corporate culture that is pervasive but often unidentifiable" (Prasso C1-2).

To Robert Brustein, writing about the toll on Heidi Holland, the collision of private and professional life simply proves that "despite the typically American hunger for total fulfillment, it's just not possible to have it all" ("Extremis" 33–34). But he fails to recognize, as the Catalyst study reveals, that Heidi and all of Wasserstein's uncommon women face corporate odds and domestic expectations frequently different from the ones men face. As Wasserstein notes, for "all the doors that have been opened for women the battle isn't over" (commencement address 1990). In particular, as Sara, Pfeni, and Heidi discover, intimacy becomes especially problematic either because it requires a near-impossible juggling act or because—in Sara's words—"some men find [them] threatening" (26).

Because *The Sisters Rosensweig* shows other avenues of middle-aged retrospective more noticeably and evinces to most a seemingly harmless tone of romance, Wasserstein's evocation of gender politics courses through the play like a noiseless current, one that nonetheless has clearly touched the lives of Sara and Pfeni especially. The undertow, however, has far from drowned them. Despite the impasse, this "unlikely trio of gladiators" have shown through their extraordinary careers and inexhaustible tenacity that they can survive quite well on their own, and though a number of insecurities ail them at the play's beginning, they not only renew and "reinvent themselves," says Wasserstein, with "some help from their sometimes-misguided but loving siblings" (Hodgins, "Southern California" 8), but also prove that, though sisterhood may have failed Heidi, it is not dead. "Husbands and boyfriends come and go, parents pass away and children leave the nest," says Melanie Kirkpatrick, "but sisters don't let you down" (A11). Huddling together on the sofa near the end of the play, they realize that, even though one "moment of pure, unadulterated happiness" seems problematic (96), by bonding "as siblings, they can anticipate a more promising future" (Gussow, "Comedy" C3).

Ending the play with this sentiment achieves two things. On one hand, it makes *The Sisters Rosensweig* Wasserstein's "valentine to her family" (Finn 366). Though she denies that it depicts the sisters Wasserstein — "part real, part made up," she says — the play's director, Dan Sullivan, states that "the family dynamic portrayed in the play is very similar" (Miller H8). "We've always been supportive of each other," said Sandra Meyer in 1993 (Hoban 34), sort of like a "permanent T-Group.... Me and my sisters" (Saline 91).

Finally, though it examines among other things the role of men in women's lives, *The Sisters Rosensweig* ultimately celebrates "the idea of women passing on the torch of their womanhood" (Greene 33). As the granddaughter of Esther Malchah, Sara returns to Ciechocinek, Poland, and by "deciding how to put bread on the tables of those who had so blithely driven them all away," she says, "I couldn't help but see it all as a minor triumph for the women ... in my mother's faded photographs." In the same vein, one can appreciate Pfeni's decision to write of other women's plight in Afghan villages and Tajikistan as a corollary and fitting tribute to the harsh conditions under which her grandmother and the other "lucky few had escaped with false passports" (80). Finally, as daughters of Rita Rosensweig, a woman who, according to family legend, "could make the Cossacks run away" (106), Sara, Pfeni, and Gorgeous "learned gumption at their mother's knee" and continue to foster their matriarchal tradition of resilience through unabashedly affectionate sisterhood (Greene 33).

For now, the one carrying the torch at the end of the Rosensweig line is Tessie Goode. She is Sara's daughter, Pfeni's "kindred spirit" (Stuart 63), and, as everyone "always told me," says Sara, "just like Rita" (106). Though Tessie has also come to a crossroads in her life, trying to determine her place in the world as a nonpracticing Jew and American expatriate in London, she too will survive. As Rita Rosensweig and "her stunningly brilliant daughters" have proven (95), even at middle-age there "are real possibilities in life" for uncommon women and others (106).

# 6

# What Price Glory?

[B]eing a woman is all about boundaries.
—Judith B. Kaufman to Quincy Quince
in *An American Daughter*

A man in Judith's position would never be made
to feel regretful at midlife.
—Lyssa Dent Hughes to Walter Abrahmson
in *An American Daughter*

Fix it kiddo cause it ain't getting any better.
—Judith B. Kaufman to Quincy Quince
in *An American Daughter*

Like *The Sisters Rosensweig*, *An American Daughter* focuses on the lives of middle-aged, uncommon women, and like its past two predecessors, it brings Wasserstein to another level of maturity in terms of depth and subject matter. Although it attempts to accomplish many things, the play primarily examines "the impossible choices women are forced to make," and, in particular, "the ways American society punishes them no matter what they choose" (Marks, "Outsider" H5), a task that to some extent she executes in all of her works, most typically through the consequences of her characters' attempts to confront an "either/or" scenario or to have it all. In *An American Daughter*, however, Wasserstein inverts the price—jarringly so—for whereas her other heroines won political victories at the expense of personal happiness, Lyssa Dent Hughes becomes the first whose feminist complexion, as perceived by others, exacts a professional and public price, as well as a private one.

"What intrigued me," says Wasserstein, "was the idea of women of my own generation who were successful, intelligent, coming to power and suddenly in the public arena.... I started to think about what they are allowed and what they are not allowed. I mean, if Nannygate* hadn't existed, what a great thing to make up as a way to talk about it" (Marks, "Outsider" H10). Reminiscent of Nannygate, Wasserstein's "Jurygate" (99) becomes one of her ways "to talk about it," specifically as a media-fired scandal that unravels what was expected to be "swift confirmation" (13) of an obviously qualified candidate—woman candidate, in particular—as United States Surgeon General.

To examine Lyssa's downfall in light of a contemporary American landscape, Wasserstein broadens the play with a number of subsidiary issues connected, directly or otherwise, to the main tragedy. In addition to the media's treatment of public figures and, especially, of derailed cabinet appointees Zoë Baird and Kimba Wood, Wasserstein spotlights national health care, gay culture, and spin control, as well as the centrist expediency of a thinly disguised Bill Clinton and—none too subtly—the skewering of his wife, Hillary. Most significantly, Lyssa's defeated nomination is also framed against the current state of feminism, the alleged backlash against it and the emergence of neofeminist ideologists, thereby making *An American Daughter* not only "her most ambitious work to date" (Evans 100) but also "by far her most politically pointed work" (Franklin, "Time" 64).

Despite her "agenda of important issues" (Sheward 60), Wasserstein nonetheless remains firmly on familiar turf. In her previous plays, not only did she focus primarily on how women negotiate the way between careers and private life, but, beginning with *Isn't It Romantic*, it became clear in her materialist examination of feminism's impact that few women could "have it all." At the forefront of whatever else Wasserstein wishes to accomplish in *An American Daughter*, that viewpoint still prevails.

Lyssa's dearest friend, Dr. Judith B. Kaufman, most closely typifies what usually happens to Wasserstein's heroines when situated in this context. From Lillian Cornwall, who became not only

---

*Nannygate was a scandal involving President Clinton's first attorney-general appointees. See page 109 for details.*

CARL A. RUDISILL LIBRARY
LENOIR-RHYNE COLLEGE

the first to articulate the impossibility of having it all but also a har-
binger for its resulting "either/or" paradigm, to Janie Blumberg, to
Heidi Holland, to Sara Goode and Pfeni Rosensweig, Wasserstein's
uncommon women have discovered to their dismay that choosing a
career seems invariably to compromise, among other things, one's
pursuit of everlasting love. In that tradition, illustrating again her
cultural-feminist tendency to recycle ideas, Wasserstein reprises the
cost of that choice through Judith, a 42-year-old African American, who gives the play the kind of middle-age retrospect found in
*The Sisters Rosensweig*.

A professor of oncology at Georgetown Medical School and
senior physician at its breast cancer unit, Judith is to her distress also
single and childless. Previously married to a man now living in Seattle with a male lover, she has most recently undergone a "five-year
cycle of great expectations and regret" (11) in an attempt to become
pregnant through in vitro fertilization and hormone treatment.

At first glance, Judith's failure at matrimony and pregnancy
seems simply to be the result of choosing the wrong man, especially
since a homosexual husband would presumably account for limited
opportunities to conceive. Ironically, to add insult to injury, Judith's
ex-husband and his companion have begun adoption procedures,
leading Judith to wail to Morrow McCarthy, the play's gay conservative and a stand-in target for Judith's resentment, that she wants
her "time back" (30). Common sense dictates, however, that not
only did Judith undoubtedly have a sexually active relationship with
the man for at least a period of time but she also could have remar-
ried, making her former situation only part of the reason for, in
particular, her childlessness.

As dramatic convention, this set-up has more to do with Wasserstein's desire to create an uncharacteristically dubious mouthpiece
regarding gay—and, specifically, gay male—culture. Given the bitter circumstances of her past, Judith is a natural for this, an acerbic
vent for viewpoints that, along with the play's delineation of Morrow as a "bit of a villain" (Linda Winer, "Angry" B2), contrast
sharply with the earlier, sympathetic portrayals of Peter Patrone
and Geoffrey Duncan. "Has it ever occurred to you," Judith says to
Morrow, for instance, "that you and many of the brightest and most

CARL A. RUDISILL LIBRARY
LENOIR-RHYNE COLLEGE

creative minds in this country have been waylaid into a preposterous position that puts forward sexual preference as the reason for all personal and societal happiness." More to the point, she says, there "won't be national health insurance or decent schools because of where you choose to place your penis" (25).

To some extent, Judith's observation acts in tandem with Lyssa's health care agenda, but Wasserstein's uncustomary dart at gay men seems squarely directed and deliberate. It is accompanied, furthermore, by a double-edged anger fueled by Judith's work in breast cancer—underfunded, on the one hand, in research, but undersupported, on the other, by gay men who to Judith seemingly enjoy far greater succor from women in the AIDS epidemic. Positing the devastation of breast cancer as a corollary to the specter of AIDS, she asks Morrow, "Do you know how many AIDS benefits I've been to? Do you know how many donations I've made? But I am still waiting for one gay man to voluntarily come to my hospital and say 'I'm concerned about a disease that's decimating my mother, my aunts, and my sister'"(30).

Beyond Wasserstein's political implications, however, and despite Judith's admittedly disastrous marriage, what realistically has had much more than anything else to do with Judith's putting off motherhood is, as she herself knows, her medical career. Essentially, the birth of a child would have compromised her profession, with or without the help of a husband, and now, at 42, her so-called biological clock shows signs of being ticked out. "I can't believe I let the time go by," she tells Lyssa, and despite being "a remarkable doctor" (9) she regrets "never having children" and "never having learned to be a woman." In short, she tells Lyssa, "I've wasted my life"(58).

Judith makes this admission at the climax of her misery near the end of Act 1. As with *The Sisters Rosensweig*, Wasserstein frames *An American Daughter* to coincide with a specific event, in this case, the period between Rosh Hashanah and Yom Kippur generally known as the Jewish New Year. A practicing Jew, or—in the words of Quincy Quince, the play's irritatingly pithy neofeminist— a "walking Crown Heights" (33), Judith has just returned in this scene from an observance of Holy Taschlich, the Festival of

Regrets marked by casting crumbs, which symbolize one's sins and grief, out to sea. Drenched and crying, Judith admits to Lyssa that, momentarily crazed during services by the so-called failures of her life, she leapt on impulse into the Potomac River. Though it never sounds like a serious suicide threat, it indicates the depth of her frustration, making both the tearful scene and the inconsolable Judith into Wasserstein's "most poignant depiction of middle-aged regret" (Evans 100).

According to Lloyd Rose, Judith's "valuable medical work" (D5) makes it inconceivable that she would suffer so much angst over childlessness. As *The Heidi Chronicles* showed, professional success cannot always dispel yearning for certain kinds of private fulfillment, and, as Rose himself demonstrates, some people simply cannot fathom the importance women frequently attach to motherhood and, specifically here, to biological motherhood. The point Wasserstein wants us to grasp, however, is not what Judith chose but that she felt she had to choose. Specifically, she had postponed childbearing for a career while facing the kind of "either/or" deadlock Wasserstein repeatedly dramatizes, only to wish later that she had chosen family life or, more likely, had attempted to have it all. At play's end, she learns that her time has run out: Judith will never get pregnant. She comes to terms with that—convincingly so—but not before Wasserstein makes it known, in her materialist feminist mode, that a "man in Judith's position would never be made to feel regretful at mid-life." More specifically, as Lyssa tells her husband, no "successful male believes his options are over at 42. A man can always start again" (17), including—before, during, or after his career—the pursuit of fatherhood.

Unlike Judith, Lyssa at the onset of *An American Daughter* appears to be the first uncommon woman finally to upend Lillian Cornwall's "either/or" legacy. Married with two children to a seemingly nice man, not only is she a "professor of public health at Georgetown" but at 42 she also "runs a major public hospital" and serves as "president of the National Women's Health Association" (50). Lyssa, in other words, has it all, including a nomination to the post of Surgeon General and a nod from *Time* as one of the "fifty top leaders over forty" (41).

Though the audience does not immediately know all this, Wasserstein makes it clear as soon as the curtain rises that Lyssa's world consists fully of a family life and the extraordinary career to go with it. Before even a word of dialogue is spoken, we see Lyssa as she's "picking up toys, balls" and other items in an obviously well-appointed domestic setting, while simultaneously we hear her giving a health care speech from a television set in the background (1). To achieve the balance of both worlds, explains Lyssa, "I am generally overcommitted and slightly hysterical" (37), though "I'd prefer to be someone who didn't always feel compelled to make such an obvious effort" (47). Working hard to keep her self-possession, she indeed "has it all," says Nancy Franklin, "only to find that others want to take it away, for no better reason than that they can" ("Time" 68).

Though Franklin generally pinpoints the impulse that defeats the nomination, Wasserstein intimates early that at least one part of Lyssa's world, her marriage to Walter Abrahmson, shows signs of trouble with or without the interference of others. When feminist author Quincy, for example, introduces herself to Lyssa as Walter's former student and dubs him "the only man who 'gets it,'" Lyssa replies tartly that Quincy is "much kinder to him than I am" (2). Walter himself does not appear until the second scene, and although he and Lyssa experience a little tryst with each other at the end of it, Wasserstein makes the sexual and ideological tension between them fairly clear.

Despite appearing proud and supportive of Lyssa's nomination, for instance, Walter irritates her repeatedly in this scene by undermining her politics. "[Y]ou're trapped in some self-righteous mishmash of the past," he says. "You're not even curious anymore" (21). As a counterpoint, he considers the more youthful Quincy and Morrow "refreshing" (17) and "original" (19) cultural newcomers who are "looking directly at the future" (21).

This scene also reveals that their sex life is according to Lyssa "very low risk" and "really a distance problem" (18), circumstances that probably make her suspect Walter would prefer a younger woman. The signs for this seem innocent enough: he simply comments on her rumpled figure and clothing, for example, and supposedly still entertains memories of having "sex with Joanie Tenzer," a girl from his high school days (16). Whatever doubt she may accord her suspicions is dispelled, however, when—with media, friends, and family brunching in their home—Lyssa catches him kissing Quincy at the end of the next scene.

Though a Harvard graduate and "distinguished Mellon Professor of Sociology at Georgetown" (32), Walter at 42 finds himself "deep in a mid-life identity crisis" (Brantley C11). Known largely for his book, *Towards a Lesser Elite*—"a standard text in over three thousand colleges," he claims (18)—Walter lately has been featured in "Where Are They Now" columns (18), and has become a self-described "also-ran" in magazine lists that feature his wife as one of the nation's major policy players (41). In short, between Lyssa's nomination and his own falling star, Walter has begun to feel "that the times have passed him by" (Rose D5).

When Quincy asks him pointedly whether he's happy, Walter offers in response that he lives "in one of the nicest homes in Georgetown. [His] wife is Ulysses S. Grant's fifth-generation granddaughter, [and his] father-in-law is [a] senator." Furthermore, his "children are both at the Sidwell Friends School ... and [his] five-year-old book is a standard for deconstructing liberalism" (42). The evidence for Walter's happiness, however, rests mainly on things other than himself and, as Greg Evans notes, his book has become "more history text than modern study" (100). Unfortunately, for both Lyssa and him, with the book "suddenly dated," his overall worth a question to himself, and the limelight increasingly centered on his wife, Walter's "panic over 'disappearing' drives him to betrayal" (Linda Winer, "Angry" B7).

Although Walter betrays Lyssa in more ways than one, as I will show later, his most obvious betrayal makes him not only foolish but also, in terms of timing, incredibly stupid and selfish. Specifically, in the midst of Lyssa's triumph and unfolding defeat, Walter sleeps with Quincy. Though Lyssa already presumes this, she never asks about it until the withdrawal of her nomination. By then, though Walter has obviously come to his senses and realizes his "terrible mistake," Lyssa recognizes that, in his vulnerable and self-absorbed condition, he blithely can and does overlook her more stunning, much-publicized defeat in order to air his own shortcomings. "[T]his was my nomination," she tells him coldly. "Can we please not make it your humiliation?" (98).

Though it remains uncertain at the end whether Walter's unfaithfulness, not to mention the stress of the wrecked nomination, will ruin their marriage, Lyssa plainly has limits to her forgiveness. In the play's first draft, Wasserstein made it clear that they would separate: Feeling blamed for offenses real and imagined, an angry Walter, in fact, initiates it. Fearing "too much overkill," Wasserstein in the stage version opts for some ambivalence (telephone interview 1997). In it, Walter himself seems to expect the worst, though, asking Lyssa outright with a mixture of apprehension and regret if she will still be home when he returns from one of his panel discussions. She will, but when he worries further if any "ghosts" lurk under their bed, Lyssa tells him frankly that "It's too early to tell" (109).

In light of Wasserstein's œuvre, Lyssa's troubles with Walter should surprise no one. As noted earlier, Wasserstein has covered this particular territory before, concluding in nearly every instance, as *The Sisters Rosensweig* chapter demonstrated fully, that for one reason or another her uncommon women do not sustain relationships with the men they love. Well-educated and at the top of her profession, Lyssa has reaped some heady benefits from a women's movement that made her options possible, and despite living with and through her success, Walter in the waning of his own career apparently feels somewhat threatened, placing the marriage in a precarious situation.

In this regard, Lyssa's circumstances resemble that of her predecessors. But what makes her—and this play—so different is that, as the usual misstep to having it all, the "probable breakdown" (telephone interview 1997) of Lyssa's marriage plays a secondary role to the play's main catastrophe; namely, that her failed nomination is, as a feminist problem, the first instance in Wasserstein's œuvre of any disintegration or private cost in the professional sphere.

Though she appears eminently qualified, Lyssa's selection by a poll-conscious Democratic president "not unlike the present White House occupant" (Marks, "Outsider" H10) comes at least in part from the perception that she represents political centrism. As one anchorman puts it, she is, according to "Capitol Hill insiders … a popular choice with both pro-choice soccer moms and more conservative fast-food dads" (13). This irks Walter considerably, primarily because he believes that despite Lyssa's "record as a brilliant health care administrator" (13), she's "being packaged as a bipartisan combination platter." More specifically, he says, Lyssa's father, a Republican senator from Indiana with conservative politics, makes her "okay with the right-wing Nazis," while her own politics make her "a pin-up for the do-gooder commies … just another example of this administration's expedient conceit that there is no more left or right, just a palpable and ineffectual center" (14).

Lyssa's politics, as Walter intimates, do not meet in the middle at all, but lean, in fact, toward what Judith calls her "bleeding heart" liberalism (4). Among other things, she bemoans "welfare reform, which will only increase the poverty of children" (28); frets about profiteering hospitals and the unchecked and dangerous side-effects of fertility treatment; and generally supports gun control, air pollution standards, more female coronary research, and reproductive freedom for women. "According to my daughter," says Senator Alan Hughes, "no individual is responsible for their own actions. A bad childhood and an underprivileged adulthood are the cause of all of society's evils" (37). Lyssa's nomination does not fail, however, as one might expect, because of specific policy agenda. It fails because some of the men in her life betray her on an oversight, while, worse, the women of America denounce her for a slip of the tongue.

The first glitch in Lyssa's appointment occurs when television interviewer Timber Tucker learns that despite her previous court appearances to plead exemption from jury duty, Lyssa failed or forgot to do anything about the latest summons, which, according to her, she misplaced. Dubbed by the press as "Jurygate"(99), the incident immediately erupts into a national scandal.

Lyssa attributes her contretemps—as well as her lack of jury service in general—to "work and family conflicts" (49) or, as she states in a televised interview, "simply bad juggling of a working mother" (91). Regardless, even she clearly realizes just how serious the fallout will be. "I've probably just set back the case for every cause I believe in," she says to Timber privately, "not to mention cast a shadow on women in government" (55).

Nearly every reviewer concurs that "Jurygate" contains "shades of Zoë Baird" (Williams D2), who along with Kimba Wood suffered the infamy of Nannygate. Though Wood technically had done nothing wrong, Baird withdrew herself from consideration as the first female attorney general when Senate Judiciary Committee hearings revealed that "she had hired two illegal immigrants from Peru to tend her son ... and had never paid Social Security taxes on their income" (Povich 47). Wasserstein, in fact, alludes to the incident twice. For one, when Timber expresses curiosity over Lyssa's nanny, Carmelita, not only does Morrow rebuff him for "sniffing up a dead end," but Quincy also declares, somewhat accurately, that the "entire Nannygate incident was an outgrowth of the 70's having-it-all mythology" (36). Lyssa's plea for understanding, furthermore, sounds very much like that of Baird, who told the committee, "I was acting more as a mother than someone who would be sitting here designated as attorney general" (Povich 47).

According to Judith, if Lyssa "were a man, this wouldn't beat road runner cartoons. It'd be a non-issue," she says, "an oversight. They'd blame it on the maid or a wife" (72). This may or may not be true, but as Walter Shapiro notes on the play's real-life Nannygate counterpart, "Perfection in all aspects of [Baird's] life was the only standard," while Stephen Breyer went on to become a Supreme Court justice despite neglecting to pay Social Security taxes for a part-time cook ("Washington" A4).

Although sexual politics, as will be discussed, contributes negatively to the overall picture, critics and characters alike generally also fault Morrow for "none too accidentally" making the jury notice an issue in the first place (Evans 100). Modeled on former *New Republic* editor Andrew Sullivan (Stearns, "Ambitious" 1D), Morrow is a political pundit and former *Washington Post* columnist, who—in Walter's prescient words—knows how to make a "more interesting spin than most people" on just about anything (19). In that vein, when Morrow reveals Lyssa's mistake during the at-home taping of Timber's "Time Zone" puff piece, which he attends as a longtime family friend who interned with Lyssa's father, he simply thinks of it as part of a lively discussion on elitism. "I was just making a point," he says. "Like writing a column" (78). Unfortunately, his example of elitism and, specifically, of "the current left-wing rage for selective privilege or self-righteous entitlement" (48) is Lyssa, and, in particular, her repeatedly citing her responsibilities as a public health administrator to escape jury duty.

Though he is universally blamed for ruining Lyssa's nomination, Morrow points out that the one who first brings up the jury debacle is, in fact, Walter. "You put it out there," he tells him (52), proving further, in Wasserstein's words, that "Walter is a mess" (telephone interview 1997). Although the taping had not yet begun, Walter reveals to everyone, including Timber, the entire story of past exemptions and the misplaced notice, referring to it further as just another instance of the "professional women's virus." Regarding the last summons, in fact, he admits to advising Lyssa "not to even open it. No professional woman of her class does" (37).

To me, not only is Walter unquestionably guilty of initiating the jury ruckus but, given his vulnerable state, he also has—consciously or not—a motive. He "should have protected her," as Morrow says to him, "and not mentioned it to begin with" (52). That Timber does not pursue the story the first time he hears it just makes Morrow the convenient scapegoat for what amounts to Walter's other betrayal in the play. Simply put, Morrow had no tale to tell without Walter's irresponsible gaffe, one that he may have inadvertently committed but one that escapes the notice and speculation of everyone except the man they blame.

Timber's failure to seize the information immediately seems at first glance either kind or inconsistent with the "duty-driven" stance he takes after the story emerges again during taping (Barnes, "No Hitting" 35). However, as a newsman who gained fame as a Gulf War correspondent modeled on "Scud Stud" Arthur Kent (Rose D5), Timber knows an off-the-record disclosure among friends and family will only elicit a denial of ever having been said or ever having happened until a lengthy investigation proves otherwise. Though he alleges disgust with "info-tainment"(27), Timber is, in fact, a news shark, a dangerous one who covers his chase with moral pretense.

As Linda Winer observes, he "cannot resist the cheap headline" (Linda Winer, "Angry" B7), and, despite a promise to do his "best to guide" Lyssa (57) through a "straightforward" follow-up (87), he makes her last interview a tough, ratings-assured event.

In short, Timber "sensationalizes [Lyssa's] comments" from the beginning (Williams D2), and singlehandedly creates the "media circus" responsible for her defeat (Sheward 60). In the aftermath of his first report, for instance, not only does Quincy unleash a series of statements and talk show appearances, but reporters also begin "camping out on [Lyssa's] doorstep" (65), tabloid-style headlines appear, and everyone else's opinions register via cyberspace and telepolls.

Though the media spectacle acts as a dramatic device to unravel Lyssa's nomination, it also gives Wasserstein an "opportunity to aim a few satiric darts at our scandal-hungry press and public" (Sheward 60). According to Dana Wood, Wasserstein feels "incensed at some of the more extreme cases of invasion of privacy—the 'Nannygate' incident involving Zoë Baird and Kimba Wood being one example" (154). Wasserstein herself ponders, "What is public life now? ... And what's a scandal and what isn't? ... What happens to someone's private life because of that? It's vicious"(Wood 156).

Wasserstein's response to this, according to Walter Shapiro, is to portray "with withering accuracy the damage wrought by the tart-tongued TV culture of Washington" ("Washington" A4). Specifically, it manifests itself in everything from Morrow's misguided commentary, to Quincy's phrasemaker-brand of observation, to the mass participation of both press and public in fueling Lyssa's downfall, to Timber's "chaos theory of broadcasting" purporting that whatever is "happening this moment won't be happening three minutes later" (96). Furthermore, as Nancy Franklin observes, at "no time during this bacchanalia of talking heads is there any serious discussion or debate of health-care issues" (Franklin, "Time" 70). The entire travesty is, in other words, emblematic of the contemporary thirst for shock versus substance, one that, coupled with the technological capacity for news-in-a-nanosecond, makes present America "the only generation that could create and destroy Lyssa Dent Hughes" (84).

Although Clive Barnes complains that the jury "situation proves unrealistically loaded" and seems far "more 'spinnable' than those which derailed Lyssa's true-life counterparts" ("No Hitting" 35), the unanswered summons that originally piques Timber's curiosity and initiates the media frenzy does not ultimately in itself force Lyssa's withdrawal. During the televised roundtable in which Morrow first wreaks his havoc, the decisive blow to her nomination occurs when Lyssa makes a throwaway remark about her mother, who died when she was 14. "I don't remember [her] having any sense of adventure at all," says Lyssa. "She was the kind of Indiana housewife who took pride in her icebox cakes and cheese pimiento canapes" (46). Reminiscent of Hillary Clinton, "who paid dearly for saying that she didn't want to stay home and bake cookies" (Franklin, "Time" 64), Lyssa's comment mobilizes the women of America into what Lloyd Rose calls "the Revenge of the Pillsbury Bake-Off Contestants" (D5).

In short, Lyssa is undone in the long run not by the jury fiasco, but by damaging opinion polls showing that women have reacted against her and have exaggerated what she said. The "huge media fuss about Mrs. Clinton's insult to cookie bakers everywhere was obviously on Wasserstein's mind," says Rose (D5), and as with the First Lady's remarks, Lyssa's make her seem "snobbish and unsympathetic" to other women (Barnes, "No Hitting" 35).

Lyssa does not initially realize, however, the extent to which women have become her real enemies. A self-described "person who can do some good, who has done a lot of good," she becomes incensed that a "goddamn misplaced slip of paper is being used to unravel all [my] possibilities" (63). As Walter points out to her, though, it is "all about the goddamn pimientos" (61), not the misplaced jury summons or, for that matter, her politics. The "women of America ... are furious with you," he says. "You're pretty ... you're admired, you're thin, and you have a great soul. Face it," he proceeds, "in the heartland that means you're one prissy privileged ungrateful to her mother, conniving bitch" (63).

Though Lyssa doubts the veracity of what Walter says, she quickly reverses her opinion when her father introduces her to Billy Robbins, a Senate spin control expert who, above all, wants Lyssa in the next interview to become "more down-home and less Bryn Mawr," or, in short, to appear more domestic and less exceptional to the women of middle America (Franklin, "Time" 70). "Talk about your mother. How much you miss her," says Billy. "Women respond to that. Make them like you" (70). To mitigate further the "Miss MD–PhD, holier than thou" (64) persona that has arisen from her publicized remarks, Billy also recommends that Lyssa avoid anything elitist or ultraliberal: "no women's lib, no high-falutin charm…. You may be a privileged person but you're also a working Mom … and on Sunday you go to church and bake cook-ies" (66). In summary, he says, "Americans want to see the wife as Marjorie Lord [Danny Thomas' television spouse] who just happens to be a doctor now" (67).

Though Lyssa protests that she "can't pretend to be someone [she's] not" (67), she truly considers herself a caring and gifted can-didate for the Surgeon General post, and, consequently, she not only agrees to apologize but also consents to wearing a "soft color attire" accompanied by a headband (70). This, of course, mimics what Hillary Clinton did in an effort to fashion herself—more to public taste—as the wife of a Presidential candidate, and to tone down the fact that the legal profession considered her to be one of the country's brightest lawyers. Ironically, the headband, in partic-ular, symbolizes for Lyssa the position in which she finds herself. "I can put it on and I can take it off," she tells Quincy. "I thought I had earned the right not to. But I still know how to appear to be a lot of things to a lot of people" (86).

Lyssa's climactic, final interview with Timber Tucker near the end of the play is, in my opinion, one of the best-written scenes in Wasserstein's œuvre. It begins as an innocuous and fabricated fam-ily-values confab consisting of Lyssa, Walter, and Lyssa's father, Senator Hughes, but with dramatic precision it evolves into what David Patrick Stearns calls Lyssa's "slow-burning defense" ("Ambi-tious" D1). Though Timber does address the jury notice, he makes it clear from the outset of his interview that the "Lyssa Dent Hughes Problem"(50) has transformed itself into one of many mainly "fem-inist maelstroms" (91).

"Female public opinion is running against you 4:1," Timber

points out to her (91). More specifically, he tells Lyssa, "Many American women feel that your private life disqualifies you from such an important humanitarian position," and with the "latest poll" indicating that they find her "condescending and elitist" (94), "women's groups, both from the left and the right" have pressured the poll–conscious President to withdraw her nomination (89).

Like Heidi Holland, Lyssa reveals a bit of idealism when she confesses surprise about the strong opposition from women. "Most of my work in medicine has been in increasing awareness of women's health issues," she says in self-defense (91). This has little to do with what generated the controversy. As Timber knows, perception counts. In an ironic upheaval of Wasserstein's mother-daughter motif, Lyssa's innocent comment about her mother marks her as a modern-day feminist who denigrates heartland values. At the personal level, therefore, Timber explains, many "women feel your attitude towards your mother is your attitude towards them" (93).

Timber's handling in this interview of the original comment that caused all the fuss is nothing short of unconscionable. It demonstrates, in fact, not only the highest level of unethical practice but also a twisted seizure of what Linda Winer calls the already "sensationalized blips America seems to love to self-destruction these days" ("Angry" B7). Having asked Lyssa if she resented her mother or felt that her mother's "horizons were limited," he goes on to wonder without basis whether Mrs. Hughes "battled substance abuse" like so "many political wives" (93). This, more than anything, finally cracks Lyssa's cooperation with Billy Robbins' spin control.

"How is this relevant to my confirmation?" she asks (93). "I don't believe we can really judge who will make the best Surgeon General based on their mother's marital happiness…. The women of America should concern themselves" with their immediate health issues—breast cancer, ovarian cancer, reproductive rights—and not, she retorts, her "father's wives," her "cooking," or whether she "did or didn't like" her mother" (94). At the end of the interview, Lyssa removes the headband, effectively ending not only the telecast and any pretense of compromise but also all hope that she will become Surgeon General.

Because of her previous achievements, Lyssa, according to

Linda Winer, allowed herself to believe that gender equity and representation had finally arrived at the point where the need to wear "headbands and bake cookies" had become obsolete and unnecessary. "As career women know too well these days," however, "she was wrong" ("Angry" B7). As Winer's analysis suggests, a dualist prescription still exists even for a powerful and successful woman like Lyssa Dent Hughes, whose rise and fall in this play comes, literally, under the personal and political influence of a women's movement whose repercussions continue to divide the nation.

Tracing the path of Lyssa's downfall makes *An American Daughter*, by far, Wasserstein's most detailed exercise in materialist feminism. Through it, she airs a number of viewpoints about the place of women in American society and, by association, the state of feminism in the nineties. Most notably, says Greg Evans, "Wasserstein pulls no punches in presenting Lyssa as a scapegoat for a country that still resents feminists—particularly successful feminists" (100). More specifically, the flack over the jury summons and the intense criticism of her throwaway line about her mother point to the "unreasonable standards to which high-profile women are held" (Stearns, "Ambitious" D1).

Wasserstein's "conversation on any given day may contain observations about the way women are seen and judged," says Nancy Franklin ("Time" 64). In general, she sees women as "perennial outsiders," and, according to Andre Bishop, believes "that no woman can really be part of the ruling class"(Marks, "Outsider" H10). Lyssa, therefore, is a "poster for [her] feelings about a country that continues to thwart its best and brightest women" (Brantley C16), a predicament that Lyssa herself clearly realizes. "There's nothing quite so satisfying as erasing the professional competency of a woman," she says at the end (95) and, unfortunately, especially in the ranks of government, "there aren't enough other women in office to pretend it doesn't matter" (86).

To some extent, such effacement manifests both sexual politics and a negation of liberal feminism's first principle of equal rights or, in this case, equal treatment. As Lyssa tells Walter when the outcry first emerges, "this would never happen to a man" (64), including—ironically—her father, who served twenty years in the Senate, eight years in Congress, and several years as a city mayor without facing public censure or moral indignation over the fact that he had married four times. It also proves, contrary to what Walter tells Quincy, that feminism should *not* "cease and desist in the twenti-eth century like Soviet communism or the rotary dial" (40). If any-thing, as Lloyd Rose so aptly observes, Lyssa's case echoes the "creepy streak of sexual nastiness in so much of the Hillary-bashing" (D5), proving not only that sexism remains very much alive but that fem-inist work remains very much incomplete.

Sexual politics aside, however, Lyssa is also victimized, as Tim-ber suggests, by "feminist backlash" (76). "For all our advances, the role of women is still a highly volatile subject," notes Quincy. On one hand, women are unfairly categorized as "beautiful but dumb, smart but neurotic," yet "in this case," she says, the "'ice box cake and pimiento canape moms' are justifiably furious at having their life choices minimized" (61). In other words, though men might cre-ate labels or resent female intrusion into their sphere sometimes, especially when a feminist undertone seems remotely present, women—as this play demonstrates—have in some cases become equally vocal proponents of the backlash.

The outcry that women unleash against Lyssa brings Wasser-stein back to the feminist difficulty she faced in *The Heidi Chroni-cles*; namely, the deterioration of sisterhood, and, more specifically, the inability of some women to embrace not only feminism but one another. In contrast to Heidi and Susan, Lyssa and Judith for the most part still support each other, but like the power shower group and locker-room women who alienated Heidi, the women of Amer-ica have shunned Lyssa. In this case, undoubtedly, they would echo the sentiments of Chubby, Alan Hughes' fourth wife, who feels compelled to state, "I'm not a quote-unquote feminist" (46).

Wasserstein, who has repeatedly stated that she is, finds it dis-concerting that women participate in feminist backlash and, by exten-sion, openly conflict with one another about the kinds of choices they make. Her own life illustrates why she feels this way. If "not for fem-inism," she says, "I would not be writing plays"(Marks, "Outsider" H10), yet her own mother—despite Wasserstein's success—has criti-cized her for not having married and started a family (Wasserstein,

*Bachelor Girls* 20). Walter, as already demonstrated, realizes first that many women see Lyssa's choices as evidence of privilege and antimotherhood, and that, conversely, Lyssa sees their choices, according to their interpretation, as marginal. As a result, they rebuke her, and, in this case, terrible consequences unfold, even though, ironically, in the play's last scene, Judith tells Walter that according to the latest "instant radio poll ... the women of America believe three to one that Lyssa was treated unfairly" (100). As this turnaround illustrates, sisterhood may not be dead but it is at best unpredictable.

In addition to the feminist concerns already cited, Wasserstein—by way of "Jurygate"(99)—not only attacks the Nannygate incident, which she considered "an insult to all women of ambition" (Marks, "Outsider" H10), but also illustrates what little sympathy, to her, a woman can expect when she fails to combine without misstep a very busy career and the ongoing demands of a household that she herself is still largely expected to fulfill.

According to Quincy Quince, "Jurygate," which she christened as the "Lyssa Dent Hughes Problem," proves that Lyssa remains a "prisoner of her gender. Specifically, she is a prisoner of her gender's and her generation's miscalculation that liberation was in fact the assumption of both her own and her opposite gender's responsibilities" (50). Since this in a roundabout way simply points to the downside of "having it all," Wasserstein, to some extent, would certainly agree. As indicated in previous chapters, she disdains what "having it all" has meant for women and believes it represents a largely impossible goal for which women either exhaust themselves or fail trying. As Lyssa tells Quincy at the close of Timber's last interview, "We're all tired of the having it all generation. Try 'the arrogance of being earnest' or 'the Antigone Defense'"(97).

Quincy herself is a troubling figure in the play, not only as the agent for Walter's infidelity but also as a rather significant centerpiece for its feminist framework. To a large extent, Quincy participates in what Wendy Kaminer cites as a philosophical problem in the women's movement; namely, that the movement itself has become "fragmented by identity politics and the proliferation of interest groups" (12). Though political conflicts among American women arise largely from antifeminism, class differences, and criticism of one another's choices, Quincy represents the kind of faction and friction Kaminer cites, politically through her rhetoric and writing, and personally, of course—in the worst betrayal of sisterhood and good sense imaginable—by sleeping with Walter, among other things.

Quincy has fashioned herself, according to Lloyd Rose, into "what one might call a Sexual Power feminist whose idea of working for a cause is to write a book" (D5). In that regard, she has arrived in Washington to promote *The Prisoner of Gender*, which has made her the "bright new star of neo-feminism" (Franklin, "Time" 63), and to reveal plans for not only a book on fathers and daughters but also, in the immediate future, a book—à la "Sexual Power" feminism—"about women restoring their sexual identity" called *Venus Raging* (34).

Sex, says Quincy, "is wildly important." As part of the identity politics Kaminer cites—in this case, one favoring "Sexual Power"—she and her twenty-something generation of young women, she tells a room full of men, "want to have some fun," and, more specifically, "want to come home to a warm penis" (34). According to Walter Shapiro, Quincy's rhetoric suggests "a miniskirted clone of feminist author Naomi Wolf" ("Washington" A4), who, among other things, "famously described her first orgasm in *The New Republic*" (Young, review of *Promiscuities* Q3). In defense, Walter says Quincy "believes she can make [feminism] new" (17), but Lyssa distrusts its "rebirth" in all of Quincy's doings (2), and, according to the way she depicts her, so obviously does Wasserstein.

For Wasserstein, Quincy is on several fronts an ersatz feminist. As a "post-feminist sexpot" (Barnes, "No Hitting" 35), she espouses the kind of ideology Maureen Dowd—who nabs a mention in the play (81)—would characterize as "bimbo feminism [that gives] intellectual pretensions to a world where the highest ideal is to acknowledge your inner slut" (A23). Quincy also exhibits an irritating penchant for what I call sound-bite feminism, one that either blatantly lacks depth or oversimplifies everything feminist into the kind of tidy phrase or pithy reflection that creates an instant media moment. Beach Boys music, she says, for instance, exemplifies the "romanticization of male sexual idolatry" (1), or the kind of "California crap … so limited in positive body imagery for women" (43). Women, she says, "wouldn't suffer from lack of self-esteem if men had more secure centers" (36). Lyssa, she says, in the current phraseology of feminist dissension, has been "re-positioned … as a victim feminist, which absurdly undermines [her] legitimacy as a power one"(62), only to declare later that Lyssa has "disenfranchised her femininity which will inevitably result in what I call … 'the good girl tragedy'"(87). Judith rightly calls it all "trumped-up trends by would-be best-selling authors" (77), trends that in Quincy's hands, says Ben Brantley, reveal a feminism "only skin deep" (Brantley C16).

Quincy's commercialized aims, sexual agenda and sound-bite pretensions alone would make her feminism problematic for Wasserstein, but, as the juxtaposition of Lyssa and Judith against the much younger Quincy demonstrates, her new guard of feminism also points to a generation gap profoundly disturbing to the playwright. Though Quincy tells Lyssa, for instance, "how grateful women of my generation are to you" and that they are "the direct beneficiaries of your battles, your disappointments, and your achievements" (8), her gratitude amounts largely to what Nancy Franklin calls "lip service to the feminists who made her career possible" ("Time" 71). Her "prisoner-of-gender" assessment of Lyssa reveals that she, in fact, believes the previous generation of feminists overwhelmed themselves trying to excel and have it all, making even "sex … just something else to be good at…. My generation wants to do it all," she explains, "but we want to have some fun too" (34). Consequently, as Lyssa points out, Quincy sees *herself* as the liberated woman "as opposed to the frigid, overextended no-fun narcissists of my generation" (53).

Disdainful of what she perceives as the mistakes of her predecessors, Quincy, in Wasserstein's eyes, lacks real insight into a feminist past that made it possible for both Lyssa and Judith—as well as Quincy—to become the successes they have. Like Lyssa, therefore, she is a poster in this play, specifically for Wasserstein's misgivings about the "attitudes of young women, who, she believes, do not understand the degree of trail-blazing that women of her generation have had to perform" (Marks, "Outsider" H10). As Nancy

Franklin notes, "it's one thing to encounter resistance to feminism—the word and the concept—from the generation ahead of you, and quite another to see the generation behind you blithely dismissing the foundation that you've built your life upon" ("Time" 71).

Another problem younger feminists like Quincy present for Wasserstein is that, to some of them, female self-identity may still need guidance in the new feminist era but gender wars are a thing of the past. As Quincy tells Judith, "I think we're at a place now when we can look beyond gender" (4). Lyssa, however, "doesn't buy into the neo-feminist notion," represented by Quincy, "that the battle is all but won" (Evans 100). Neither does Judith. Though Quincy says her mother taught her that "a woman's life can have no boundaries" (5), Judith tells her that "being a woman is all about boundaries...," adding, "Maybe you'll be one of the feminine elite—marry well, best-selling author, mother of three," says Judith (6). Maybe, in other words, Quincy will have it all and have her fun, too, without the obstacles that befell her predecessors. Judith and Lyssa—as well as Wasserstein—have grave doubts, however, and, if anything should prove to Quincy that boundaries do indeed still exist for women, it is Lyssa's downfall.

Throughout the play Quincy claims that "women's issues are my priority" (7), but, philosophical differences aside, Quincy's "only real cause," says Greg Evans, "is herself" (100). As Wasserstein delineates her, Quincy not only exudes "personal vapidity and willingness to use her female wiles" (Spencer 2), but, in the long run, with her pithy neofeminist rhetoric as proof, she is nothing more than an "opportunistic trendmeister" (Stearns, "Ambitious" D1). In short, Quincy primarily cares about self-promotion and "self-aggrandizement," to the point that she "callously exploits Lyssa Hughes' ordeal," as her flurry of television appearances and editorials illustrate, to sell books and "to forge her own camera-crazed career as a TV pundit" (Shapiro, "Washington" A4). As Lyssa herself knows, "My nomination is going to sell Quincy a hell of a lot of books" (62).

As this overview indicates, Wasserstein's feminist framework here is extensive. It includes the plight of successful women, sexual politics, feminist backlash, the disintegration of sisterhood, Nannygate, and the having-it-all syndrome. It also addresses neofeminism, the real, the imagined, the commercialized, and the generationally divisive. Altogether, therefore, *An American Daughter* emerges as another—in this case, up-to-the-minute—history of the women's movement, with Lyssa Dent Hughes, as the title suggests, indeed the daughter of its legacy. In other words, as its heir, she could carve a professional life from the options made possible by the women's movement, yet is living proof, as the failure of her Surgeon General nomination indicates, not only of feminism's divisions but also of ongoing tremors experienced by women who dare to admit, support, or profit from feminism.

Used as a catchphrase for Timber's program, the play's title, a literal reference to Lyssa's political ancestry, also brings about the revelation that despite her defeat, Lyssa will survive. As the great-great-granddaughter of Ulysses S. Grant and his wife, Lyssa's namesake Julia Dent, Lyssa has, her father notes, not only the same "tremendous reserves of strength and compassion" as her ancestors (47), but also the example of Grant himself, a great general but ill-considered President, whose "foibles are our foibles" and who stands, therefore, as a "timeless" "American hero, imperfect just like all of us" (90). In that way, Lyssa is, as Timber states, "truly an American daughter of the highest caliber" (91), one who makes an "unconditional surrender" only to her beliefs, and one whose valedictory at the play's finale recalls her great-great-grandfather's words: "You need not fear but that I will come out triumphantly"(108).

In upholding her principles, Lyssa takes her place alongside Wasserstein's other heroines as a definitive uncommon woman. As an astonishingly political play, however, *An American Daughter* itself is much riskier than its predecessors. "It *is* a watershed," admits Wasserstein (personal interview 1995). For one, though it resurrects familiar issues of choice, women's erratic support for one another, and relationships with men, it lacks the broad swath of humor that Wasserstein's other works have while doing the same thing. Unlike her previous plays, too, Wasserstein leaves the comfort of people and spaces she knows intimately, and, in their place, she confronts the less familiar anomalies of Washington politics, not only to intersect the blurred lines of America's liberal and conservative viewpoints, but also to juxtapose spin doctors, the media, and other unforeseen forces against naive counterparts like Lyssa herself and Walter.

Though the result is tense and complex, many critics found *An American Daughter* an unconvincing work of both art and civic commentary. Ranging from William Grimes' bloodless barb that "Wasserstein slipped on a banana peel with *An American Daughter*" (Weekend 2) to the more common, mixed review regarding its "wit and intelligence without much of a play" (Harris 28), critics appeared baffled or unmoved by Wasserstein's attempt to create a political gaze both subtle and overt. Stung by criticism and snubbed for all but Lynne Thigpen's Tony nomination and award for her portrayal of Judith, the play—Wasserstein's first to open on Broadway without an Off Broadway tryout (Franklin, "Time" 63)—closed after 115 performances (Speers D2).

One chief drawback for most reviewers seemed to center on the alleged lack of "any human dimension" to Wasserstein's character development (Ridley, "Nelligan" F4), and, in particular, on the attendant perception that as archetypes—the "black Jewish best friend," the "gay conservative neighbor," the "opportunistic feminist author"—they fill the stage simply to generate "a panel discussion on contemporary topics" (Sheward 60). As such, claims Michael Feingold, every character "bears a cluster of relevant buzzwords" that merely advance the positions of her or his stereotype and reveal little depth or insight into psyche or motivation ("Bypassed" 91).

Though prototypical, especially in terms of traditional character development, some of the powerbrokers in *An American Daughter* are deliberatedly designed as role-playing role-players. Though they do "tend to describe themselves in the terms of comically annotated resumes as soon as they enter a room" (Brantley C11), their actions, as Walter Shapiro points out, are "actually an apt depiction of life among the elites in Washington, where everybody immediately defines themselves in terms of their jobs, their glib opinions and their latest TV performances" ("Washington" A4).

For some, this may seem like a flimsy rationalization for characters who, in some cases, admittedly lack much dimension outside of stock identities. Quincy Quince and Morrow McCarthy are particularly conspicuous as thinly fleshed figures who serve obvious thematic purpose but evince little else; and though he makes only a brief appearance to try to salvage Lyssa's nomination, Billy Robbins' preppy demeanor as a transparent spinmeister borders on near-caricature. However, as Wasserstein's catalogue of characters demonstrates from Susie Friend and Carter to Tom Valiunus and others in between, she likes to use characters as devices to juxtapose ideas or personalities around her principals.

In *An American Daughter*, she takes an artistic risk in incorporating into a single play a higher number of types or stock devices than she usually does. This *is* a political play, nonetheless, and these characters *are* personating politically savvy people who not so ingenuously carve their words and appearances very carefully. In short, for a play that says "something about a world that reduces people to sound bites and social abstractions" (Brantley C16), Wasserstein's character depiction seems not only justified but suitable.

In some respects, and in this play especially, Wasserstein's minimalist character development has something to do with her tendency toward a cultural feminist writing style. Although she structures *An American Daughter* less episodically and more along the tighter time frame and linear design of *The Sisters Rosensweig*, the play evokes a bit of "lyric mode" by incorporating numerous concepts—or "discrete elements" (Russ, "Heroine" 12)—into a dramatic center so full that it may seem sometimes to elude clear definition. For some, this is bad writing, but in terms of feminist literary criticism, "lyric mode" historically represents a distinctive form of female literary technique. As devices, therefore, Morrow and Quincy, in particular, function less—and, therefore, succeed less—as flesh-and-blood characters, and instead perform conceptual work in what Wasserstein herself declares as a "play of ideas" (personal interview 1995).

Critics accustomed to more traditional frameworks as a benchmark of a drama's worth might understandably scoff at "lyric mode," but it also happens to shed light on what some also criticized as the play's "crowded agenda" (Feingold, "Bypassed" 91). *An American Daughter* obviously addresses several topics, some more loosely than others, that in themselves do not formally constitute what the play is about. According to Wasserstein, her work captures "the sadness of a generation," and, more specifically, says Nancy Franklin, "her generation's conduct in the political sphere" ("Time" 64). As a realistic endeavor, any literature of politics must necessarily lend itself to a diverse issues-driven machinery that, in this case, swirls around those things, from tabloid journalism to pseudofeminism, that fuel Wasserstein's own discontent and disappointment. The significance here, however, lies in the resulting stew: a fusion of not only topical items but also "disparate types" of character (Spencer 2) that altogether contribute to numerous ideas, but do not always or necessarily materialize—à la "lyric mode"—into a *theoretically* coherent presentation or one with a visible center.

As previously stated, this may seem unsophisticated to an analyst who prefers a more solid approach to the lyric one, but even if critics misunderstand, reject, or undermine Wasserstein's cultural feminist technique, especially in the aggregated landscape of *An American Daughter*, the play is actually far tighter and more integrated than credited. Some critics stated at the extreme, for instance, that *An American Daughter*'s numerous issues, characters, and "beguilingly clever remarks" clouded its plot or eliminated it altogether: "If only there were a play to go with them," complained Lloyd Rose (D1).

Rose's remark and others like it puzzle me. The play's fundamental focus is plainly Lyssa. As billed, she is the "American daughter"; and, since the purpose, just as plainly, is to show what has led to the collapse of her nomination—which Wasserstein clearly tracks—the play can settle for a single contrivance or, as it preferably does, branch into a realistic web of complications. To that end, even with its quasi-evocation of "lyric mode" and its amalgamation of self-contained parts, the fact remains that every issue cited or implied—except for gay culture, perhaps—bears certain relevance throughout Lyssa's unfolding story. The underdeveloped issues—gun control, women's reproductive rights, and the high incidence of breast cancer, to name three—might not be fully analyzed nor might their relationship to one another be clearly drawn, but the entire pot does have a single political commitment to feminism, and the pot, by and large, does touch Lyssa's life.

Though it may seem "overstuffed with lists of things to accomplish" (Brantley C11), *An American Daughter* thereby somewhat belies its own multiple abstractions. It acts somewhat like "lyric mode," but, in effect, not only do the issues accomplish their dramatic, theatrical work, but the characters themselves—an "ideological cross-section of the American political, professional and media elite" (Marks, "Outsider" H10)—set up the viewpoints and power plays. Consequently, as David Spencer points out about its complex panorama, the "mixed reactions" to *An American Daughter* may have "less to do with the quality of the play ... than [with] the skillful way in which it challenges you to react" (2).

Though Clive Barnes believes that overall the play "seems to promise more than it actually delivers" ("No Hitting" 35), *An American Daughter* does deliver a lot. As Hal Holbrook points out, Wasserstein at the very least presents several points of view (Williams D2), one example being the sympathetically drawn role of Lyssa's father, the conservative Republican senator who "jettisons ideology" (Ridley, "Nelligan" F4) to defend his liberal daughter at every turn of the play's burgeoning scandal.

Furthermore, as Walter Shapiro asserts, *An American Daughter* is, importantly, the "first play or movie to realistically convey Washington's chilling embrace of the performance values of television" ("Washington" A4), from Morrow's indiscreet showmanship, to Quincy's sound-bite intrusion into the at-home montages, to Timber's seizure and distortion of the original disclosures, to Billy Robbins' orchestration of Lyssa's hair and clothing. Finally, despite Steve Parks' belief that debates about "whether women can 'have it all'" seem "dated" and "tiresome" (B7), it also breaks new ground about the "marginalizing of competent women" (Ridley, "Nelligan" F4) like Lyssa, who in her own words "really wanted that job" (98) and lost it—ostensibly because of an oversight, yet ultimately because of the unrealistic expectations made of her as a woman nominee.

"I thought I would write something that would make some people uncomfortable," says Wasserstein (Marks, "Outsider" H5-10). Therein lies, perhaps, the trouble. As Linda Winer, who unequivocally found the play "bright, eloquent and great-hearted," notes, *An American Daughter*, with its political forces, critical gaze, and feminist control, could not have been written fifty years or five years ago. Yet, predictably, even in contemporary times, she says, critics would accuse Wasserstein of being "too dogmatic," "too angry," "too mean to young people," and "too stuck in her previous worries about … discredited liberalism and feminism" ("Angry" B2).

Wasserstein, I believe, took an interesting gamble with *An American Daughter*. Though its relatively short Broadway run, along with the adverse reaction of some critics, may eventually relegate the play to a minor movement in both her career and theatre history, I prefer, nonetheless, to judge it as Linda Winer has: "From events where others have found confusion and impotent rage, Wasserstein has made sense and dramatic art—all wrapped in truth-is-stranger-than-fiction absurdities so precise they could serve some day as a time capsule from our baffling time" ("Angry" B2).

# 7

# Fem–en(act)ment Revisited

Although the Wasserstein œuvre as I have presented it contains just five major plays, her numerous essays, film scripts, and other minor dramas, as well as the proliferation of awards she has won, indicate that she not only maintains high visibility but also possesses, at least in some circles, a fairly strong reputation. Despite Wasserstein's achievements, however, only a few minor works have been anthologized, and her material is seldom listed in the thousands of course syllabi distributed to university literature classes every year. Though Wasserstein's "triple whammy" (personal interview 1995) undoubtedly contributes to these omissions and not only excludes her from serious academic consideration but also precludes her from taking her place in the esteemed canon, I believe, especially in the context of fem–en(act)ment, that Wasserstein distinguishes herself as one of the most important writers in contemporary American literature.

Although several factors impinge on Wasserstein's inclusion in the canon, some critics attribute her absence, in part, to the perception that, with only five major plays in approximately twenty years, she does not seem like a very prolific *playwright* (Miller H8). This viewpoint is misleading and sidesteps the fact that Wasserstein writes prodigiously in other media. For instance, in addition to being a contributing editor for *New Woman* and *Harper's Bazaar*, a position she once held with the now-defunct *New York Woman*, she has written a screen adaptation of Stephen McCauley's *The Object of My Affection* that was slated for theatrical release in 1998, and is currently working with Disney television for a two-hour, Cy Coleman musical of her 1996 children's book, *Pamela's First Musical* (telephone interview 1997). Also under development are both a

BBC series and a film to be directed by Daniel Sullivan based on *The Sisters Rosensweig*; a childhood memoir of Brooklyn for Sonny Mehta, editor-in-chief of Knopf (telephone interview 1997); and, scheduled for November 1999, a telefilm for ABC's "The Millennium Project," a Hallmark Entertainment endeavor which has commissioned Wasserstein and other American playwrights to "draw on the theme of the coming millennium" (Carter C18), and for which, Wasserstein says whimsically, she may write about "shopping on Mars" (telephone interview 1997). Clearly, as this snapshot of only one brief period in her life indicates, the scope of her literary repertoire and the immense level of productivity are nothing short of impressive.

More importantly, however, in answer to the critics who find her theatrical output underwhelming, Wasserstein has also produced a number of lesser-known minor dramas, some of which even contain the feminist undercurrent, subtle or otherwise, found in her major works. Playwrights Horizons in 1973, for example, staged *Any Woman Can't*, whose principal character, says Wasserstein, "is sort of a prelude to Janie and Harriet." After failing a dance audition, the heroine—with shades of Harriet more than of Janie—"sort of gives up and marries someone she doesn't love" (personal interview 1995). She also collaborated with Christopher Durang in another early feminist-based work, *When Dinah Shore Ruled the World*, presented at the Yale Cabaret in 1975. "About role models," says Wasserstein, it depicts four women in a beauty pageant and, like *Any Woman Can't*, interacts with another Wasserstein play by including the "emotional life" of Holly Kaplan, who mistakenly becomes a pageant contestant (personal interview 1995).

In addition, Wasserstein has written the one-act play *Tender Offer*, presented by the Ensemble Studio Theatre in 1983; *The Man in a Case*, also a one-act play, staged by the Acting Company in 1986; "Smart Women, Brilliant Choices," a segment for the production of *Urban Blight* at the Manhattan Theatre Club in 1988; and two other Playwrights Horizons productions, *Happy Birthday, Montpelier Pa-zazz* in 1976, and the failed 1986 musical *Miami*. Most recently—even as *An American Daughter* was playing Broadway—Wasserstein wrote another feminist-inspired piece called *Workout*, a short monologue anthologized in 1997 in *Plays for Actresses* that somewhat resembles Heidi Holland's long soliloquy and lampoons the having-it-all syndrome Wasserstein loves to skewer.

Although the canon to which Wasserstein's works aspire itself has no clear membership or standard of excellence, admission to it, as with any exclusive club, appears mainly to reflect the preferences of those who select and the essence and longevity of those who already belong. As Jill Dolan asserts, in terms of ideology—both structural and cultural—the canon generally "expands its ranks only for those works that already resemble its historical members," a condition perpetuated in part, she says, because the "invisibility of both its constructors and the origins of its construction render the canon peculiarly (but purposefully) remote from question or attack" (*Feminist Spectator* 32, 31).

Tying together both research and conjecture, Jane Tompkins in *Sensational Designs* examines the canonization of Nathaniel Hawthorne, for instance, and concludes that his position as a literary lion seemingly originated not so much from artistic merit but from the combination of savvy salesmanship, nepotism, and the good-old-boys' network, and it maintains itself, she purports, largely through subsequent generations of academics reluctant to risk ridicule by questioning his preeminence. At the heart of her work, Tompkins wants mainly to demonstrate how writers like Hawthorne have benefited—and still do benefit—from privileges and literary codes removed from women's experience. Ultimately, therefore, like Dolan, she believes that institutionalized cultural and literary ideology has led historically to the canonization of somewhat divergent imitators and, with few exceptions, to the marginalization of those on the peripheries of that ideology.

For Dolan and Tompkins, the ideology in question is patriarchal. This assumption may or may not be true, but I suspect that the governing ideology for literary style and substance is, nonetheless, traditional. For dramatists, then, a work whose formula resembles the Aristotelian model for structural unities and tragic hero probably makes critics and academics more attuned to its potential merits than, say, one with Wasserstein's tendency toward episodic construction and women characters who make life-choices. "Though women are often said to write 'small tragedies,'" she says in self-defense, "they are *our* tragedies, and therefore large, and therefore legitimate" (Betsko 426). From a traditional, critical perspective, however, neither the style nor the substance of those tragedies belongs to the tradition of Shakespeare, Miller, or Williams, and when critics fail to appreciate alternative forms of drama or to acknowledge "female systems of signification" such as Wasserstein utilizes, they tend to dismiss the underlying meanings of the work and to render it marginal or noncanonical (Dolan, *Feminist Spectator* 20).

Dolan believes that only "a shift in the gender of the spectator ... will fundamentally disrupt the construction of the canon" (*Feminist Spectator* 39). I agree, but only to a point. Some of the spectators who still subscribe to traditional assumptions about what makes good writing and good drama are, after all, women, and some of them find Wasserstein's works, for instance, entertaining but not aesthetically satisfying in terms of their sometimes cinematic structure and tragicomic content. The shift needed to diversify the canon, therefore, lies not in gender but in critical practices.

In the case of women's literature, feminist literary criticism in particular has loosened traditional analytic approaches not only to reconstruct literature by women and deconstruct literature by men about women but also to develop methodologies suitable for evaluating it all. The field is, however, still, relatively speaking, new, especially with regard to drama, so that as Dolan points out, even feminist reviewers feel trapped between praising and critiquing works "against a standard that is yet to be defined in the balance between ideology and art" (*Feminist Spectator* 36).

Feminist literary critics do largely agree on this, however: the canon—that is, if one believes in the necessity of a canon at all—must make room for more diverse measures to include not bad work but different work. Without diversification, Wasserstein faces particularly challenging circumstances for canonical inclusion. On one hand, despite being philosophically interesting and creative, she does not, as Dolan would say, resemble her predecessors. Secondly, compared to novelists, dramatists—and especially those who, like Wasserstein, work in a comedic vein—tend to be underrepresented in the canon altogether and women dramatists, in particular, are rendered nearly invisible. As Wasserstein herself reflects, theatre is "not the mainstream of American culture" (Wood 156), a situation somewhat in her mind with *Pamela's First Musical*, which she hopes will "inspire" a new "generation of theatregoers" (Heffley 71).

Whether or not one regards the canon itself as too politically and culturally prescribed to be of use, the quest for fair, artistic evaluation still remains, one that must advocate not only variant criteria but also the notion that critics and academics become "responsive to *and resistant to* text and performance in ways that are still difficult to conceive" (Mandl 126; emphasis added). For her part, Tompkins has abandoned the "question of literary value" based on "asking whether a work is unified or discontinuous, subtle, complex, or profound," because those criteria represent to her the ideology that helps to stigmatize certain works. Instead, her critical modus operandi first relates a text "to the historical circumstances and the contemporary cultural discourse to which it seems most closely linked" and then asks if the text achieves its aims and whether the aims have any value (38). "I see [texts] as doing a certain kind of cultural work within a specific historical situation," she says, and "as providing society with a means of thinking about itself." Essentially, therefore, she replaces the traditional critical perspective that judges the merit of a work by its "attempts to achieve a timeless, universal ideal of truth and formal coherence" with one that accentuates its purpose and cultural framework (200).

In the quest to devise new measures for critical assessment, fem–en(act)ment represents my contribution to feminist literary criticism as a contextual way to study women's theatre and, in this case, to establish Wendy Wasserstein as a major dramatic figure. Wasserstein's plays *are* fem–en(act)ment: theatrical works guided by a feminist disposition that thematically and stylistically enact situations of interest to women, the psychological and social effects of which form the core of her drama.

What makes Wasserstein's dramas particularly significant in terms of fem–en(act)ment is the effect they achieve collectively. Although they do not quite replicate the entire life cycle, they read all together like the ages of woman. Her heroines graduate from college, pursue careers, and reach middle age in a pattern that makes her works sometimes seem like sequels to one another. "Maybe they do react to the previous plays," says Wasserstein. Although she adds facetiously that they must seem "like a prolonged manic episode" (personal interview 1995), they present a profound picture of the main idea Wasserstein wants to enact: the impact of the women's movement on private life.

To explore that impact, Wasserstein examines and re-examines the same themes and motifs in nearly every play: careers, mother-daughter relationships, sisterhood, the relationships between uncommon women and the men they love, and the prices they pay through it all. *Every* play ultimately is about choices, however, and from her uncommon women to Lyssa Dent Hughes, every choice has an almost inextricable connection to feminism, especially in terms of the possibilities—as well as difficulties—it has created, and the life it has carved between career and family. Age changes the perspective, but ultimately the question simply shifts from "Where am I going?" to "Where have I been?" and "What has it meant?"

In terms of the issues so important to her, *The Sisters Rosensweig* represents a thematic tour de force for Wasserstein. The sisters are her uncommon women, roughly twenty to thirty years older, still grappling with the impact of the women's movement. In retrospect, Pfeni at 40 continues to review her career options like Kate Quin and company. Gorgeous attempts to have it all. Sara and Tessie resurrect the mother-daughter battlegrounds that Wasserstein initiated with Janie and Tasha Blumberg. The sisters discover the sisterhood that eluded Heidi Holland, and the prospect for loving, sustained relationships with men remains as problematic as it did for Kate, Janie, and Heidi.

By returning to the same concerns and showing their impact at different stages, Wasserstein effectively utilizes the cyclic strategy associated with feminist-inspired writing, a strategy she applies to the feminist theoretical implications in her work as well. The liberal feminist perspective throughout the collection comes about by virtue of Wasserstein's emphasis in every play on the process or consequences of making choices, especially as she insists that women—uncommon women, in particular—have both the prerogative and the competence to pursue a professional life on equal footing with men. That they seemingly cannot balance their careers with romance or marriage in the same way as men, however, comprises the focus of her materialist feminist mode. Though she never resolves the conundrum regarding this balance, she manifests its causes, development, or repercussions in each play and recognizes it in her own life as well. "Right about now we'd be divorced and sitting at opposite ends of the temple during the bar mitzvah," she says of her own near-encounter with marriage, "and I probably wouldn't have written most of my plays" (Kennedy 64).

Wasserstein's observations about herself regarding career and marriage exemplify the influence of her own experiences on the theoretical and thematic conditions of her plays. On the whole, the works do not really create strict autobiography, even with the many doses of private memory and family-based characterization, but her tone and viewpoint are clearly autobiographical and theoretically typical, as well, of cultural feminist literature. Although Wasserstein's mother-daughter paradigm and emphasis on female friendship also reflect cultural feminism, its most evident manifestation lies in the nonlinear, episodic style that she recycles in all but *The Sisters Rosensweig* and *An American Daughter*.

If *The Sisters Rosensweig* represents Wasserstein's thematic tour de force, then *The Heidi Chronicles* represents her theoretical tour de force. Heidi's conviction that "all people deserve to fulfill their potential" (181), the sentiment that lies at the heart of both the play and her work in general, is ostensibly a slogan for liberal feminism. Scoop's ultimatum that it is "either/or" (202), on the other hand, provides the framework for Wasserstein's materialist feminist inquiry, while the autobiographical nuances, consciousness-raising scene, sisterhood theme, and Heidi's decision to adopt, along with the play's wildly episodic and sweeping panorama of personal and political history, all together make *The Heidi Chronicles* an absolute gem of cultural feminist theatre and sensibility.

Despite the theoretical and thematic gravity of her depiction of feminism's impact on private life, Wasserstein defuses it with a "Mask of Humor" (Barney 50), one that she exercises with such mastery that theatre critics who evaluate her work as performance drama tend to write profusely about her "very large gift for being funny" (Eder 48) and—especially—about her instincts for dispensing "witty observations and smart one-liners" (Watt, "Sisters" 77). According to Howard Stein, this tactic diminishes her stature as a playwright. Since even "grief in Wasserstein's plays ... [is] handled in the spirit of dark comedy and black humor," he says (25), her comic style becomes a "camouflaging element," and, consequently, by not "providing the script with the seriousness that their subjects" deserve, her convictions are rendered to near-invisibility (24).

Though I agree with Stein that Wasserstein's humor damages her appeal to the serious analyst, I do not agree that it prevents her from enacting the issues she wants to explore, and, therefore, I consider the bias against her unfounded. In the case of *The Sisters Rosensweig*, for example, Clive Barnes deemed its seriocomic formula as "Anton Chekhov reincarnated as a mixture of Neil Simon and Woody Allen" ("Wendy's Wonderful" 24). Likewise, Phoebe Hoban called it "Mary Tyler Moore meets Chekhov" (34). The point is this: a play requires far more than the presence of three sisters to earn even the remotest comparison to Chekhov, a conventionally acclaimed *serious* dramatist who—like Wasserstein—"had the objectivity to mock his characters' flaws and delusions ... [and] the sympathy to portray their hopes and sorrows" (Kozikowski 453) while utilizing "the comic, the absurd or the eccentric" (Pitcher 13).

Because Wasserstein knows what reviewers have said of her comic tendencies, Nancy Franklin believes that in *An American Daughter* she "seems to be answering the critics who find her social humor too glib." To some degree, the playwright herself seems reluctantly to confirm this. "Part of me gets angry," she says. "I think, You want not funny? You want to know what's under here? You want not the jokes? There are not jokes here" (Franklin, "Time" 70). The humor does not disappear in *An American Daughter*, but it does seem "more pointed" (Evans 100). In other words, it seems more directly attached at any given moment to precisely the point she wishes to present. Quincy's sound bites appear ridiculously funny, for instance, because she herself and her quasifeminist ideas *are* ridiculous to Wasserstein. Similarly, even when the humor functions as a means of ironic deflection, the way it does for Janie Blumberg and Wasserstein herself, it targets a very particular aspect of the character's motivation. Judith's "humor is her anger" (Franklin, "Time" 68), says Wasserstein, a way of dealing with Morrow, for example, as a phantom of her own disappointing marriage.

Despite this seemingly deliberate development in *An American Daughter*, Wasserstein to her credit has always maintained an awareness of the delicate scale on which all her plays develop. The "trick," she says, is "to find the balance" between humor and bathos (*Rosensweig* x). I think she succeeds in achieving that equilibrium, perhaps most noticeably in *The Heidi Chronicles* and *An American Daughter* but, in counterpoise to the critics who sometimes accentuate the comedy more, I have chosen throughout this study to engage in a counterbalancing act myself by not quite ignoring her humor but by neutralizing it against her more serious aims.

Interestingly, Wasserstein regards the way her plays "relate in style and structure" specifically in terms of how she handles their bathetic and comic tone. "I think they skip a generation," she says. "*Uncommon Women and Others* and *The Heidi Chronicles* are comedic, but not from a comedic vein. *Isn't It Romantic* and *The Sisters Rosensweig* have a boulevard comedy structure. It's the difference between comedy versus a play of ideas" (personal interview 1995). Obviously, the politically explosive *An American Daughter*, in following *The Sisters Rosensweig*, continues this tradition of alternating her uses of humor, especially since—conversely—she plans to make its successor a light romance or farce tentatively titled *Old Money* (telephone interview 1997).

According to Wasserstein, of all the plays she has written thus far, *An American Daughter* is the achievement of which she is most proud. "I think it's my best play," she says (telephone interview 1997). Though "still comedic," it "goes darker" than any of her previous work, creating with its deeply political, issue-driven plot and less autobiographical flavor nothing short of a milestone in her career (personal interview 1995).

Most importantly, in terms of the theoretical and thematic implications of fem-en(act)ment, *An American Daughter* also moves Wasserstein forward in her feminist disposition. It keeps her design, leitmotifs, and pluralist, ideological complexion intact, but as a darker vehicle in her repertoire, it not only contains her most sweeping consideration of feminism but also raises the stakes of feminism's impact. Janie loses Marty, Heidi loses sisterhood and Scoop, and the Rosensweigs lose inner peace, but Lyssa loses her nomination. In the end, having failed to become Surgeon General and, in all probability, to save her marriage, she may appear undaunted and undiminished, but one feels her losses more unnervingly, perhaps, than those of her predecessors because of how public those losses are.

As I detailed extensively in the preceding chapter, Wasserstein also contemporizes her feminist disposition in this play by directly framing the ongoing impact of the women's movement against its current polarization. For one, though Lyssa's downfall attests in the words of Quincy Quince that women *are* prisoners of their gender, Quincy herself blatantly practices, despite an occasional insight, the current rage for a best-seller feminism that, in her case, is not a declaration of feminism, says Wasserstein, but an "aberration" of it (telephone interview 1997).

Beyond her commercial aims, though, Quincy pretends to espouse the new feminism, one not only distanced from the feminist mystique of Lyssa's generation but also less geared toward gender disputes and more inclined, presumably, to self-empowerment. Though, philosophically, this may simply be another class of feminist theory or a more progressive form of it, critics believe its proponents fail not only to decipher both the ongoing alliance between the personal and political, and the precarious relationship between private and professional desire, but also to recognize the continuing bombardment, from both men and women, upon those who call themselves feminists.

The new feminism is, then, somewhat problematic to Wasserstein, especially in the way it fuels her long-brewing concern for the way she thinks the current generation seems to view feminism historically. What "really worries her," says Sharon Elder, "is that nowadays too many younger women neither understand nor appreciate the issues that gave birth to feminism in the first place" (26). As Mary Ann Glendon notes, though some women distance themselves from their "strange brew" of aggressiveness and "rigid party line" on family and sexuality, second-wave feminists, "to their everlasting credit, broke new ground in the economic and political spheres" that the current generation would otherwise not have (A7). Quincy may believe it is "up to my generation to make feminism into a positive experience again" (First Draft 29), but given her highly visible and successful career, she provides living proof that the "emancipations of 1970s feminism live on" (Glendon A7).

More to the point, the emancipations live on in Wasserstein. As Nina Burleigh says, her "success on Broadway is proof ... that the efforts of the women's movement have borne fruit" (8). For Wasserstein, feminism begins to make choice possible. It certainly made her choice to become a playwright possible, even though she warns that as "long as you can go into a room in Hollywood and someone says, 'I can't make it, it's about girls' ... it's not over" ("Have It All?" 216).

Perhaps not. But Wasserstein has still given American drama—and American literature—something it never had: not only a body of work about uncommon women but also a character model, the uncommon woman herself, who at last counterbalances masculine archetypes like Hemingway's code hero. The œuvre might not reflect the experiences of all women in her audience, but they "often seem to emerge with a common feeling ... [that] she's on our side" (Span G1). It might not reflect the dramatic traditions of the canon, but with few predecessors to imitate, it could not and should not. It might not triumph with critics who judge drama by its tragic pulse and so-called universal appeal, but it succeeds under a new critical vision called fem–en(act)ment.

It is her own, and, as the chronicler of uncommon women, Wendy Wasserstein knows why it must proceed: "*Nulla res melior feminae re,*" she says, "or, very roughly, there's no business like women's business" ("Heidi Chronicled" 132).

# Appendix:
# New York City and
# Television Production
# History of the Major Plays
# of Wendy Wasserstein

## UNCOMMON WOMEN AND OTHERS

Opened on 21 November 1977
Presented by the Phoenix Theatre at the Marymount Manhattan Theatre in New York City
Directed by Steven Robman

Televised in May 1978
Presented by PBS Great Performances
Directed by Steven Robman and Merrily Mossman

Revived in October 1994
Presented by Second Stage Theatre at the Lucille Lortel Theatre in New York City
Directed by Carole Rothman

## ISN'T IT ROMANTIC

Debuted in earlier version on 28 May 1981
Commissioned and presented by the Phoenix Theatre at the Marymount Manhattan Theatre in New York City
Directed by Steven Robman

Opened in revised version on 15 December 1983
Presented by Playwrights Horizons in New York City
Directed by Gerald Gutierrez

## THE HEIDI CHRONICLES

Opened on 12 December 1988 after workshop performances at
  the Seattle Repertory Theatre in April 1988
Presented by Playwrights Horizons in New York City
Directed by Daniel Sullivan

Moved to the Plymouth Theatre on Broadway on 9 March 1989
Produced in association with Playwrights Horizons by the Shu-
  bert Organization, Suntory International Corp., and James
  Walsh.
Directed by Daniel Sullivan

Televised on 15 October 1995
Produced by TNT
Directed by Paul Bogart

## THE SISTERS ROSENSWEIG

Opened on 22 October 1992 after workshop performances at the
  Seattle Repertory Theatre in April 1992
Presented by Lincoln Center Theatre at the Mitzi E. Newhouse
  Theatre
Directed by Daniel Sullivan

Moved to Barrymore Theatre on Broadway in March 1993
Directed by Daniel Sullivan

## AN AMERICAN DAUGHTER

Opened on 13 April 1997 after workshop performances at the
  Seattle Repertory Theatre in summer 1996
Presented by Lincoln Center Theatre on Broadway at the Cort
  Theatre
Directed by Daniel Sullivan

SOURCES OF INFORMATION

Credits, PBS telecast of *Uncommon Women and Others*
Credits, TNT telecast of *The Heidi Chronicles*
*Current Biography Yearbook 1989*
*Playbill* (1994), Lucille Lortel Theatre, *Uncommon Women and Others*
*Playbill* (1997), Cort Theatre, *An American Daughter*
The Heidi Chronicles *and Other Plays*
*The Sisters Rosensweig*

# Bibliography of Works by Wasserstein

*Arranged as follows: Published Plays; Books; Articles; Speeches; Interviews; Unpublished Manuscripts; Performances; Teleplays and Videotapes*

## Published Plays

*Isn't It Romantic.* New York: Dramatists Play Service, 1984.
*Jill's Adventure in Real Estate or, I Can Get It for You at 3.2. New Yorker* 16 Oct. 1995: 170–77.
*Tender Offer. Literary Cavalcade* 37, 2 (Nov. 1984): 26–29.
*The Heidi Chronicles.* New York: Dramatists Play Service, 1990.
*The Heidi Chronicles and Other Plays.* New York: Harcourt, 1990.
*The Man in a Case. Orchards.* New York: Knopf, 1986. 19–31.
*The Sisters Rosensweig.* New York: Harcourt, 1993.
*Uncommon Women and Others.* New York: Dramatists Play Service, 1978.
*Uncommon Women and Others: A Play about Five Graduates of a Seven Sisters College Six Years Later.* New York: Avon, 1978.
*Workout. Plays for Actresses.* Eds. Eric Lane and Nina Shengold. New York: Vintage, 1997. 607–11.
And Terrence McNally. "'The Girl from Fargo': A Play." *New York Times* 8 March 1987: Arts and Leisure, 5+.

## Books

*Bachelor Girls.* New York: Vintage, 1991.
*Pamela's First Musical.* Illustrations by Andrew Jackness. New York: Hyperion, 1996.

# Articles

"Backlash Blues." *Harper's Bazaar* May 1993: 76+.

"Chic Love." *Harper's Bazaar* Oct. 1993: 112+.

"Christmas in Camelot." *New York Times Magazine* 22 Dec. 1996: 49.

"Confessions of a Former Fat Person." *New York Woman* Dec. 1991/Jan. 1992: 76–77.

"Confronting the Beauty Mystique." Review of *The Power of Beauty*, by Nancy Friday. *Time* 8 July 1996: 70.

"Design for Living." *Life* Dec. 1992: 99.

"Designing Men: Architects in Movies." *New Yorker* 1 May 1995: 96.

"Diary." *Slate* (30 Sept. 1996): 7pp. Online. Internet. 24 Jan. 1997.

"Don't Tell Mother." *New Yorker* (Special Women's Issue) 26 Feb./4 March 1996: 196+.

"Family Plot." Review of *Among the Ginzburgs*, by Ellen Pall. *New York Times Book Review* 2 June 1996: 24.

"Fifty Things to Do in 50 Days." *Time* 18 Nov. 1996: 122.

"First Ladies Get Dressed." *New Yorker* (*Politics Issue*) 21–28 Oct. 1996: 192.

"Franny at Fifty." *Harper's Bazaar* Aug. 1992: 42–44.

"Giving In to Gluttony." *Esquire* July 1986: 60–61.

"Heidi Chronicled." *New Yorker* 6 March 1995: 132.

"How's He Doing?" Review of *Murder at City Hall*, by Edward I. Koch with Herbert Resnicow. *New York Times Book Review* 8 Oct. 1995: 23.

"Joseph Papp." *New York* 25 April 1988: 106–08.

"Just Say No: For Most Women It's Not as Easy as It Sounds." *New Woman* 1 Jan. 1995: 47–48.

"Mad Men: The New Politically Pissed-Off Majority." *New Woman* 1 March 1995: 66+.

"Meryl Streep Comes Calling." *Saturday Evening Post* 1 July 1989: 50+.

"Move Over Waifs, the Bulge Look Is Here." *Harper's Bazaar* 1 Nov. 1993: 86.

"My Dinner with Andre (and Hillary and Bill)." *Harper's Bazaar* Jan. 1994: 38–39.

"My Low-Fat Dinner with Jamie Lee Curtis." *New Woman* 1 Nov. 1995: 50+.

"My Man Pesci." *Harper's Bazaar* Aug. 1992: 48+.

"New York Theater: Isn't It Romantic?" *New York Times* 11 Jan. 1987: H1+.

"Of Human Baggage." *Lear's* 1 Nov. 1992: 84–85.

"Party Animals." *New York Times Magazine* 20 Oct. 1996: 71.

"Party of One: Is It Un-American to Be Childless?" *Slate* (13 Sept. 1996): 3pp. Online. Internet. 24 Jan. 1997.

"Poles Apart." *Harper's Bazaar* July 1993: 40–41.

Review of *Sense and Sensibility*. Screenplay by Emma Thompson. Dir. Ang Lee. Prod. Columbia. Based on Jane Austen's *Sense and Sensibility*. *Premiere* Feb. 1996: 17–18.

"Seriously Steve Martin: A Wild and Crazy Guy? Think Again." *New Woman* 1 July 1995: 68+.
"She Saw Through Us." *New York Times Magazine* 29 Dec. 1996: 36–7.
"Shopping." *Lear's* Nov. 1993: 31–32.
"Shopping with Him." *Gentlemen's Quarterly* March 1988: 196+.
"The Itch to Get Hitched." *Mademoiselle* Nov. 1981: 146.
"The Mario Chronicles." *House and Garden* May 1991: 76+.
"The Me I'd Like to Be." *New Woman* 1 Dec. 1994: 67–68.
"The Must That Mewed: Remembering a Calico Cat." *New Woman* 1 April. 1995: 84+.
"The Princess Brides." *New York Times Magazine* 24 Nov. 1996: 92.
"Tipper Gore: More than Just a Perfect Woman." *New Woman* 1 Jan. 1996: 34–35.
"To Live and Diet." *American Health* Nov. 1992: 104.
"Way Off Broadway with Pamela." *New York Times Book Review* 30 June 1996: 35.
"Wendy's Workshop." *New York Times Magazine* 25 Dec. 1995: 37.
"Winner Take All." *Performing Arts* 1 Sept. 1990: 30+.
"Women Beware Women: When Female Friendships Go Awry." *New Woman* (Special Issue: 25th Anniversary Edition) Oct. 1995: 80–82.
"You Can't Get a Man with a Gun, *But* ..." *Cosmopolitan* Feb. 1997: 98.

# Speeches

"A Life in the Theater." The Free Library of Philadelphia. Philadelphia, 9 May 1995.
Mount Holyoke Commencement Address. Mount Holyoke College, 27 May 1990.

# Interviews

"CA Interview." By Jean W. Ross. *Contemporary Authors* Vol. 129. Ed. Susan M. Trosty. Detroit: Gale, 1990. 455–57.
Interview. By Jan Balakian. *Speaking on Stage: Interviews with Contemporary American Playwrights*. Eds. Philip C. Kolin and Colby H. Kullman. Tuscaloosa: University of Alabama Press, 1996. 379–91.
Interview. By Leslie Jacobson. *The Playwright's Art: Conversations with Contemporary American Dramatists*. Ed. Jackson R. Bryer. New Brunswick, N.J.: Rutgers University Press, 1995. 257–76.
*Interviews with Contemporary Women Playwrights*. Eds. Kathleen Betsko and Rachel Koenig. New York: Beech Tree Books/Quill Editions, 1987. 418–31.

Personal Interview. 19 Aug. 1995.

"Playwright Wendy Wasserstein Discusses Her New Book." By Liane Hansen. *Weekend Edition—Sunday.*

National Public Radio. WNYC, New York. 28 April. 1996.

"'Table for Two.' Matthew Broderick and Wendy Wasserstein." By Robert Siegel. *All Things Considered.* National Public Radio. WNYC, New York. 14 February 1996.

Telephone interview. 22 July 1997.

"Uncommon Women: An Interview with Wendy Wasserstein." By Esther Cohen. *Women's Studies: An Interdisciplinary Journal* 15,1 (1988): 257–70.

"Wasserstein Enjoys Banner Year with *The Heidi Chronicles.*" By Lu Stone. *Mount Holyoke Now* Spring/Summer 1989: 1–4.

## Unpublished Manuscripts

*An American Daughter.* First Draft. Unpublished ms. Sept. 1995.

*An American Daughter.* Rehearsal Script. Unpublished ms. Feb. 1997.

*Antonia and Jane.* Adaptation of screenplay by Marcia Kahan. Unpublished ms. Sept. 1994.

*Happy Birthday, Montpelier Pa-Zazz.* Unpublished ms. LD 7096.6, Supplementary #1, Box 1. Wendy Wasserstein Papers. Mount Holyoke College Library/Archives, South Hadley, Mass.

*How to Marry a Millionaire Part Two, or She Did So Well.* Unpublished ms. LD 7096.6, Supplementary #1, Box 1. Wendy Wasserstein Papers. Mount Holyoke College Library/Archives, South Hadley, Mass.

*Maids in America.* Unpublished ms. LD 7096.6, Box 2 and Supplementary #1, Box 3. Wendy Wasserstein Papers. Mount Holyoke Library College/Archives, South Hadley, Mass.

*Miami.* Unpublished ms. LD 7096.6, Supplementary #2, Boxes 2–3. Wendy Wasserstein Papers. Mount Holyoke College Library/Archives, South Hadley, Mass.

*Mutz.* Unpublished ms. LD 7096.6, Supplementary #1, Box 3. Wendy Wasserstein Papers. Mount Holyoke College Library/Archives, South Hadley, Mass.

*Smart Women/Brilliant Choices* (a scene from *Urban Blight*). Unpublished ms. LD 7096.6, Box 1. Wendy Wasserstein Papers. Mount Holyoke College Library/Archives, South Hadley, Mass.

*The Heidi Chronicles.* Unpublished ms. LD 7096.6, Box 4, Folder 8. Wendy Wasserstein Papers. Mount Holyoke College Library/Archives, South Hadley, Mass.

*The Heidi Chronicles.* Notebook. LD 7096.6, Box 3, Folder 1. Wendy Wasserstein Papers. Mount Holyoke College Library/Archives, South Hadley, Mass.

*The Heidi Chronicles*. Notebook. LD 7096.6, Box 3, Folder 4. Wendy
    Wasserstein Papers. Mount Holyoke College Library/Archives, South
    Hadley, Mass.
*Uncommon Women and Others*. Unpublished, updated ms. 14 Oct. 1994.
And Terrence McNally. *The Queen of Mabababwe*. Unpublished ms. LD
    7096.6, Box 1. Wendy Wasserstein Papers. Mount Holyoke College
    Library/Archives, South Hadley, Mass.

# Performances

*An American Daughter*. Dir. Daniel Sullivan. With Kate Nelligan, Lynne
    Thigpen, Peter Riegert, Hal Holbrook, and Penny Fuller. Cort The-
    atre, New York. April. 1997.
*The Heidi Chronicles*. Dir. Daniel Sullivan. With Christine Lahti and David
    Hyde Pierce. Plymouth Theatre, New York. Dec. 1989.
*The Sisters Rosensweig*. Dir. Daniel Sullivan. With Jane Alexander, Made-
    line Kahn, Frances McDormand, and Robert Klein. Mitzi E. New-
    house, New York. Nov. 1992.
*Uncommon Women and Others*. Dir. Carole Rothman. With Stephanie
    Roth, Mary McCann, Julie Dretzin, Haviland Morris, and Jessica
    Lundy. Lucille Lortel Theatre, New York. Oct. 1994.

# Teleplays and Videotapes

*Emerging Playwrights—with Wendy Wasserstein and Corinne Jacker*. Dir.,
    prod., ed. Bruce Goldfaden. Insight Media, 1976. Video, 30 min.
*The Heidi Chronicles*. Dir. Paul Bogart. Prod. Leanne Moore. With Jamie
    Lee Curtis, Tom Hulce, Peter Friedman, and Kim Cattrall. TNT,
    1995.
*Uncommon Women and Others*. Dir. Steven Robman and Merrily Mossman.
    Prod. Phylis Geller. With Jill Eikenberry, Alma Cuervo, Swoosie
    Kurtz, Ellen Parker, Meryl Streep, and Ann McDonough. *Theater in
    America*. Great Performances. PBS, 1978.

# Bibliography of
# Critical Works and Reviews

*Arranged as follows: Uncommon Women and Others; Isn't
It Romantic; The Heidi Chronicles; The Sisters Rosensweig; An American Daughter; Miscellaneous*

## *Uncommon Women and Others*

Beaufort, John. "A Wry Reunion." *Christian Science Monitor* 30 Nov. 1977.
   *New York Theater Critics' Reviews*. Off Broadway Supplement IV. Vol.
   38, No. 22. Eds. Joan Marlowe and Betty Blake. New York: Critics'
   Theater Reviews, 1977. 140.
Carlson, Susan L. "Comic Textures and Female Communities 1937 and
   1977: Clare Boothe and Wendy Wasserstein."*Modern American
   Drama: The Female Canon*. Ed. June Schlueter. Rutherford: Fairleigh
   Dickinson University Press, 1990. 564–73.
Christiansen, Richard. "A Most 'Uncommon' Playwright." *Chicago Tribune*
   24 March 1978: Sec. 4, 4.
Eder, Richard. "Dramatic Wit and Wisdom Unite in *Uncommon Women
   and Others*." *New York Times* 22 Nov. 1977: 48.
Franklin, Nancy. "McNally Men, Wasserstein Women." *New Yorker* 14
   Nov. 1994: 129–31.
Gates, Anita. "Today Most Are in Their 40s, and Pretty Amazing." *New
   York Times* 16 Oct. 1994: H5, 40.
Kalem, T. E. "Stereotopical." *Time* 5 Dec. 1977: 111.
Newton, Edmund. "'Women' One Can't Forget." *New York Post* 22 Nov.
   1977: 22.
O'Connor, John J. "*Uncommon Women and Others* on TV Tonight." *New
   York Times* 24 May 1978: C24.
Simon, John. Review of *Uncommon Women and Others. New York* 7 Nov.
   1994: 102.
_____. "The Group." *New York* 12 Dec. 1977: 103–04.

"*Uncommon Women and Others*." *TV Guide* 24 May 1978: A-83.

Watt, Douglas. "Holyoke Hen Sessions." *New York Daily News* 22 Nov. 1977: 27.


## *Isn't It Romantic*

Barnes, Clive. "*Isn't It Romantic*: and It's Funny, Too." *New York Post* 16 Dec. 1983. *New York Theater Critics' Reviews*. Off Broadway Supplement IV. Vol. 44, No. 18. Eds. Joan Marlowe and Betty Blake. New York: Critics' Theater Reviews, 1983. 70.

Corliss, Richard. "Broadway's Big Endearment." *Time* 26 Dec. 1983: 80.

Gussow, Mel. "New 'Romantic' by Wendy Wasserstein." *New York Times* 16 Dec. 1983: C3.

Kakutani, Michiko. "A Play and Its Author Mature." *New York Times* 3 Jan. 1984: C8–9.

Nightingale, Benedict. "There Really Is a World beyond 'Diaper Drama.'" *New York Times* 1 Jan. 1984: H2+.

Oliver, Edith. Review of *Isn't It Romantic*. *New Yorker* 26 Dec. 1983: 68.

_____. "The Day before the Fifth of July." *New Yorker* 22 June 1981: 86–87.

Parks, Steve. "From Wendy Wasserstein's Album." *Newsday* 10 October 1996: B7.

Review of *Isn't It Romantic*. *Variety* 17 June 1981: 84.

Simon, John. "Failing the Wasserstein Test." *New York* 29 June 1981: 36+.

Sirkin, Elliott. Review of *Isn't It Romantic*. *The Nation* 18 Feb. 1984: 202.

Watt, Douglas. "*Isn't It Romantic*: Sometimes." *New York Daily News* 16 Dec. 1983. *New York Theater Critics' Reviews*. Off Broadway Supplement IV. Vol. 44, No. 18. Eds. Joan Marlowe and Betty Blake. New York: Critics' Theater Reviews, 1983. 69–70.


## *The Heidi Chronicles*

Arthur, Helen. "I Am Woman … Sorry." *Nation* 16 Oct. 1995: 443–44.

Austin, Gayle. Review of *The Heidi Chronicles*. *Theatre Journal* 42 (1990): 107–08.

Barnes, Clive. "Hello, I'm the Me Generation." *New York Post* 12 Dec. 1988. *New York Theater Critics' Reviews*. Vol. 50, No. 5. Eds. Joan Marlowe and Betty Blake. New York: Critics' Theater Reviews, 1989. 332–33.

Beaufort, John. "Bright Facades and Serious Insights." *Christian Science Monitor* 16 Dec. 1988: 24.

Brustein, Robert. "Women in Extremis." *The New Republic* 16 (April 1989): 32–34.

"Can 'The Heidi Chronicles' Have It All?" *Vanity Fair* Oct. 1995: 216.

Gerard, Jeremy. Review of *The Heidi Chronicles. Variety* 9-15 Oct. 1995: 38.

Gold, Sylviane. "Circle Pins to Power Lunches." *Wall Street Journal* 16 Dec. 1988: A13.

Gussow, Mel. "A Modern-Day Heffalump in Search of Herself." *New York Times* 12 Dec. 1988: C13.

Henry, William A. "Way Stations." *Time* 20 March 1989: 90.

Hodgson, Moira. Review of *The Heidi Chronicles. The Nation* 1 May 1989: 604–06.

Kennedy, Dana. "Playing 'Heidi' Go Seek." *Entertainment Weekly* 13 Oct. 1995: 64.

Keyssar, Helene. "Drama and the Dialogic Imagination: *The Heidi Chronicles* and *Fefu and Her Friends.*" *Modern Drama* 34,1 (March 1991): 88–106.

Kissel, Howard. "'Heidi' Grows Up, With Grace." *New York Daily News* 12 Dec. 1988: 35.

———. "'Heidi' Lights Up Broadway." *New York Daily News* 10 March 1989. *New York Theater Critics' Reviews.* Vol. 50, No. 5. Eds. Joan Marlowe and Betty Blake. New York: Critics' Theater Reviews, 1989. 335.

Kramer, Mimi. "Portrait of a Lady." *New Yorker* 26 Dec. 1988: 81–82.

Kroll, Jack. "The Uncommon Wendy Wasserstein Goes to Broadway." *Time* 20 March 1989: 76–77.

Leonard, John. "Defining Women." *New York* 16 Oct. 1995: 70–71.

Lipson, Karin. "The Heidi Question." *New York Newsday* 30 Jan. 1989: Part II, 12–14.

Mandl, Bette. "Feminism, Postmodernism, and *The Heidi Chronicles.*" *Studies in the Humanities* 17,2 (Dec. 1990): 120–28.

McGuigan, Cathleen. "The Uncommon Wendy Wasserstein Goes to Broadway." *Newsweek* 20 March 1989: 76–77.

O'Connor, John. "An A-Plus Woman, Downbeat and Feeling Stranded." *New York Times* 13 Oct. 1995: D18.

Richards, David. "The Life and Loves of 'Heidi.'" *Washington Post* 14 March 1989: E1+.

Robins, Corinne. "Betrayals." *The American Book Review* 11.5 (Nov.-Dec. 1989): 4.

Rose, Phyllis Jane. "Dear Heidi: An Open Letter to Dr. Holland." *American Theater* Oct. 1989: 29.

Rothstein, Mervyn. "After the Revolution, What?" *New York Times* 11 Dec. 1988: Sec. 2, 1+.

Shapiro, Walter. "Chronicler of Frayed Feminism." *Time* 27 March 1989: 90–92.

Simon, John. "Jammies Session." *New York* 27 March 1989: 66+.

———. "Partial Autobiographies." *New York* 2 Jan. 1989: 48–49.

Span, Paula. "Uncommon Wendy and Her Broadway 'Chronicles.'" *Washington Post* 12 March 1989: G1+.

Stearns, David Patrick. "Lively, Liberated Heidi." *USA Today* 10 March 1989: 5D.

Wallach, Amei. "Drawing Life from Women Artists." *New York Newsday* 30 Jan. 1989: 13.

Watermeier, Daniel J. "The Search for Self: Attachment, Loss, and Recovery in *The Heidi Chronicles.*" *Staging Difference: Cultural Pluralism in American Theatre and Drama*. Ed. Marc Maufort. New York: Peter Lang, 1995. 351–62.

Watt, Doug. "This 'Heidi' Is Quite a Character: Second Thoughts on First Nights." *New York Daily News* 23 Dec.1988. *New York Theater Critics' Reviews*. Vol. 50, No. 5. Eds. Joan Marlowe and Betty Blake. New York: Critics' Theater Reviews, 1989. 331.

Weales, Gerald. "American Theater Watch, 1988-1989." *The Georgia Review* 43,3 (Fall 1989): 573–85.

Winer, Laurie. "Christine Lahti as an Angry Heidi in 'Chronicles.'" *New York Times* 9 Oct. 1989: C13+.

Winer, Linda. "Real People with Tough Questions." *New York Newsday* 12 Dec. 1988: 7+.

Winfrey, Lee. "*The Heidi Chronicles*: A Feminist in Search of Happiness (Play's Also a Prize on TV)." *Philadelphia Inquirer: TV Week* 15-21 Oct. 1995: 6–7.

# *The Sisters Rosensweig*

Barnes, Clive. "'Sisters' Makes the Big Move to B'way." *New York Post* 19 March 1993. *New York Theater Critics' Reviews*. Vol. 54, No. 4. Eds. Norma Adler, et al. New York: Theater Critics Reviews, 1993. 72–73.

_____. "Wendy's Wonderful 'Sisters' Three." *New York Post* 23 Oct. 1992: 24.

Brustein, Robert. "The Editorial Play." *The New Republic* 7 Dec. 1992: 32–34.

Feingold, Michael. Review of *The Sisters Rosensweig. Village Voice* 3 Nov. 1992. *New York Theater Critics' Reviews*. Vol. 54, No. 4. Eds. Norma Adler, et al. New York: Theater Critics Reviews, 1993. 84.

Gerard, Jeremy. Review of *The Sisters Rosensweig. Variety* 26 Oct. 1992. *New York Theater Critics' Reviews*. Vol. 54, No. 4. Eds. Norma Adler, et al. New York: Theater Critics Reviews, 1993. 70–71.

_____. Review of *The Sisters Rosensweig. Variety* 22 March 1993. *New York Theater Critics' Reviews*. Vol. 54, No. 4. Eds. Norma Adler, et al. New York: Theater Critics Reviews, 1993. 71.

Greene, Alexis. Review of *The Sisters Rosensweig. Theater Week* 5 April 1993: 32–33.

Gussow, Mel. "Wasserstein: Comedy, Character, Reflection." *New York Times* 23 Oct. 1992: C3.

Harris, William. "Hoping to Fill a Broadway House? Call Wasserstein." *New York Times* 13 Feb. 1994: 5+.

Henry, William A. "Reborn with Relevance." *Time* 2 Nov. 1992: 69–70.

Hodgins, Paul. "Southern California Theatres Host a New Breed of Female Hero." *Orange County Register* 19 Aug. 1994: 8.

_____. "Wendy Wasserstein and Mariette Hartley on *The Sisters Rosensweig*." *Orange County Register* 13 July 1994: 7.

Jafferies, Desiree. "The Ties That Bind: Soul-searching with the Rosensweigs." *OutNOW!* (2 April 1996): 2pp. Online. Internet. 24 Jan. 1997.

Kirkpatrick, Melanie. "Theater: Trio of American Plays Rooted in Reality." *Wall Street Journal* 29 Oct. 1992: A11.

Kissel, Howard. "Family Circus: Wasserstein Turns 'Sisters' into a Jovial Juggling Act." *New York Daily News* 23 Oct. 1992: 47.

_____. "Sharpened 'Sisters' Act: Move to B'way Stresses Issues, Keeps Laughter." *New York Daily News* 19 March 1993. *New York Theater Critics' Reviews*. Vol. 54, No. 4. Eds. Norma Adler, et al. New York: Theater Critics Reviews, 1993. 74.

Kraft, Daphne. "Wasserstein's 'Sisters Rosensweig' a Pungent Comedy." *North Jersey Herald and News* 26 March 1993: B7.

Kroll, Jack. "You Gotta Have Heart." *Newsweek* 2 Nov. 1992: 104.

Kron, Joan. "All-Consuming Art." *New York Times* 6 Dec. 1992: V12.

Oliver, Edith. "Chez Rosensweig." *New Yorker* 2 Nov. 1992: 105.

Richards, David. "Wendy Wasserstein's School of Life." *New York Times* 1 Nov. 1992: H5-6.

Robins, J. Max. "'Sisters Rosensweig' and Nepotism at CBS." *Variety* 4–10 Dec. 1995: 6.

Simon, John. "Not Quite Art; Not Quite Shaw." *New York* 5 April 1993: 84–85.

_____. "The Best So Far." *New York* 2 Nov. 1992: 100–01.

Specter, Michael. "Funny? Yes, But Someone's Got to Be." *New York Times* 8 April 1993: C1+.

Stearns, David Patrick. "'Sisters' Is a Kind, Clever Wasserstein Chronicle." *USA Today* 23 Oct. 1992: 4D.

Stuart, Jan. "If Chekhov Sisters Had Lived in Brooklyn." *New York Newsday* 23 Oct. 1992: 63+.

Vellela, Tony. "Wasserstein Play Is Strong on Comedy, Weak on Depth." *Christian Science Monitor* 5 Nov. 1992: 13.

Watt, Doug. "'Sisters': From Newhouse to New Home on B'way." *New York Daily News* 30 Oct. 1992. *New York Theater Critics' Reviews*. Vol. 54, No. 4. Eds. Norma Adler, et al. New York: Theater Critics Reviews, 1993. 77.

_____. "Wasserstein Pens a Pointed Drawing-Room Comedy." *New York*

*Daily News* 30 Oct. 1992. *New York Theater Critics' Reviews*. Vol. 54, No. 4. Eds. Norma Adler, et al. New York: Theater Critics Reviews, 1993. 77.

Winer, Linda. "'Sisters' Inhabit House Simon Built." *New York Newsday* 19 March 1993. *New York Theater Critics' Reviews*. Vol. 54, No. 4. Eds. Norma Adler, et al. New York: Theater Critics Reviews, 1993. 76.

## *An American Daughter*

Barnes, Clive. "No Hitting Below the Beltway." *New York Post* 14 April 1997: 35.

Bernson, Misha. "Wasserstein Comedy to Sub for 'Royal Family' at the Rep." *Seattle Times* (7 Feb. 1997): 2pp. Online. Internet. 31 March 1997.

Brantley, Ben. "In the Hostile Glare of Washington, the Media Define and Defy." *New York Times* 14 April 1997: C11, C16.

Evans, Greg. Review of *An American Daughter*. *Variety* 14–20 April 1997: 100.

Feingold, Michael. "Bypassed Hearts." *Village Voice* 22 April 1997: 91.

Harris, Mark. Review of *An American Daughter*. *Entertainment Weekly* 20 June 1997: 28.

Haun, Harry. "Trying to Coax Meryl Streep Back to Broadway." *Playbill Online* (17 June 1996): 2pp. Online. Internet. 31 March 1997.

Marks, Peter. "An Outsider Goes Inside the Beltway." *New York Times* 23 March 1997: H5, H10.

Review of *An American Daughter*. *Entertainment NY 1 News* (14 April 1997): 1p. Online. Internet. 6 May 1997.

Ridley, Clifford. "Kate Nelligan, Hal Holbrook Brighten 'American Daughter.'" *Philadelphia Inquirer* 15 April 1997: F4.

Rose, Lloyd. "Wasserstein's 'Daughter': Thin and Flighty." *Washington Post* 14 April 1997: D1, D5.

Shapiro, Walter. "In Washington, Life Imitates Broadway." *USA Today* 16 April 1997: 4A.

Sheward, David. Review of *An American Daughter*. *Back Stage: The Performing Arts Weekly* 18–24 April 1997: 60.

Speers, W. "Newsmakers: On the Boards." *Philadelphia Inquirer* 25 June 1997: D2.

Spencer, David. Review of *An American Daughter*. *AISLE SAY New York* (1997): 2 pp. Online. Internet. 4 May 1997.

Stearns, David Patrick. "Wasserstein's Ambitious 'Daughter' Scores Political Points." *USA Today* 14 April 1997: 1D.

"Washington Witness." *New York Times* 13 April 1997: H4.

Wickens, Barbara. "Nelligan's Return." *MacLean's* 28 April 1997: 10.

Williams, Jeannie. "Wasserstein's Playful Pokes at Washington." *USA Today* 15 April 1997: 2D.

Winer, Linda. "Angry and Beautiful: Brilliantly, Funnily, Wasserstein Returns to Politics." *Newsday* 14 April 1997: B2, B7.

# Miscellaneous

Albright, Patricia. Personal interview. 27 July 1995.

Backes, Nancy. "Wendy Wasserstein." *Notable Women in American Theater.* New York: Greenwood, 1989. 901–03.

Barney, Lee. "Hot Ticket." *Spotlight Magazine* March 1993: 48–54.

Bernard, Joan Kelly. "Loving, Laughing, Fighting, and Sharing It All." *Newsday* 20 Feb. 1996: B19.

Black, Kent. "The Wendy Chronicles." Review of *Bachelor Girls*, by Wendy Wasserstein. *Harper's Bazaar* March 1990: 154+.

Breslauer, Jan. "The Backstage Alchemist." *Los Angeles Times* 19 May 1996: Calendar, 3.

Burleigh, Nina. "The Wendy Chronicles." *Chicago Tribune* 21 Oct. 1990: Sec. 6, 1+.

Carlson, Margaret. Review of *Bachelor Girls*, by Wendy Wasserstein. *Time* 16 April 1990: 83.

Carter, Bill. "TV Notes: Playwrights in a Millennial Mode." *New York Times* 16 April 1997: C18.

Christy, Marian. "Everywoman—in Glittering Lights." *Holyoke Transcript-Telegram* 3 March 1990: 10.

Donahue, Richard. "Opening Night." Review of *Pamela's First Musical*, by Wendy Wasserstein. *Publisher's Weekly* 22 April 1996: 31.

Elder, Sharon. "The Wendy Chronicles." *Yale Alumni Magazine* May 1990: 24–29.

Finn, William. "Sister Act." *Vogue* Sept. 1992: 360+.

Frank, Glenda. "The Struggle to Affirm: The Image of Jewish-Americans on Stage." *Staging Difference: Cultural Pluralism in American Theatre and Drama.* Ed. Marc Maufort. New York: Peter Lang, 1995. 245–57.

Franklin, Nancy. "The Time of Her Life." *New Yorker* 14 April 1997: 62+.

Grossberg, Michael. "Close to Home." *Columbus Dispatch* 23 April 1995: D1+.

Heffley, Lynne. "Private Lives: Family." Review of *Pamela's First Musical*, by Wendy Wasserstein. *Los Angeles Times* 5 May 1996: Calendar, 71.

Heiferman, Marvin, and Carole Kismaric. "Wendy Wasserstein." *Talking Pictures.* San Francisco: Chronicle Books, 1994. 96–8.

Hirsch, Diana. Review of *Bachelor Girls*, by Wendy Wasserstein. *School Library Journal* Aug. 1990: 177.

Hoban, Phoebe. "The Family Wasserstein." *New York* 4 Jan. 1993: 32–37.

Hubbard, Kim. "Wendy Wasserstein." *People Weekly* 25 June 1990: 99+.

Kozikowski, Thomas. "Wendy Wasserstein." *Contemporary Authors* Vol. 129. Ed. Susan M. Trosty. Detroit: Gale, 1990. 452–55.

Krupp, Charla. "Women of the Year, 1989." *Glamour* Dec. 1989: 154–55.

Levis, Georgette. "Hit Playwright Has Local Connections." *Manchester Journal* 22 March 1989: no pag.

Matuz, Roger, ed. "Wendy Wasserstein." *Contemporary Literary Criticism Yearbook 1989*. Vol. 59. Detroit: Gale, 1990. 218–227.

Miller, Judith. "The Secret Wendy Wasserstein." *New York Times* 18 Oct. 1992: H1+.

Moritz, Charles, ed. "Wendy Wasserstein." *Current Biography Yearbook 1989*. New York: H. W. Wilson, 1990. 610–3.

O'Donnell, Owen, ed. "Wendy Wasserstein." *Contemporary Theatre, Film, and Television*. Vol. 8. Detroit: Gale, 1990. 449.

"Of Plays About Politics and Politicians at Play." *New York Times* 6 Oct. 1996: H5–H6.

O'Haire, Patricia. "Wasserstein's Women." *New York Daily News* 12 March 1989: no pag.

Oliver, Edith. Review of *Tender Offer*. *New Yorker* 13 June 1983: 98.

"Our Bodies No More: Four Storytellers Share Their Visions of a Post-Roe America." *Glamour* Aug. 1992: 228+.

Quinn, Judy. Review of *Bachelor Girls*, by Wendy Wasserstein. *Library Journal* 15 March 1990: 98.

Stein, Howard. "Wasserstein Reconsidered." *Theater Week* 31 Oct. 1994: 22–25.

"Women Playwrights: Themes and Variations." *New York Times* 7 May 1989: H1+

Wood, Dana. "Wendy City." *W* May 1997: 154–6.

# Bibliography
## of General Works

Abel, Elizabeth, ed. *Writing and Sexual Difference*. Chicago: University of Chicago Press, 1982.

Atkinson, Jane Monnig. "Review Essay: Anthropology." *Signs* 8 (Winter 1982): 236–58.

Austin, Gayle. *Feminist Theories for Dramatic Criticism*. Ann Arbor: University of Michigan Press, 1990.

Beatts, Anne. "Can a Woman Get a Laugh and a Man, Too?" *Mademoiselle* Nov. 1975: 184.

Benstock, Shari, ed. *Feminist Issues in Literary Scholarship*. Bloomington: Indiana University Press, 1987.

Brater, Enoch, ed. *Feminine Focus: The New Women Playwrights*. New York: Oxford University Press, 1989.

Brown, Janet. *Feminist Drama: Definition and Critical Analysis*. Metuchen, N.J.: Scarecrow, 1979.

Burke, Kenneth. *The Philosophy of Literary Form*. New York: Vintage, 1961.

Butler, Judith. "Performance Acts and Gender Constitution: An Essay in Phenomenology and Feminist Theory." *Theatre Journal* 40 (Dec. 1988): 519–31.

Campbell, Karlyn Kohrs. "The Rhetoric of Women's Liberation: An Oxymoron." *The Quarterly Journal of Speech* 59 (Feb. 1973): 74–86.

Carelli, Richard. "Study Finds Sexism in Law Schools." *Philadelphia Inquirer* 4 Feb. 1996: A5.

Case, Sue-Ellen. *Feminism and Theater*. New York: Methuen, 1988.

\_\_\_\_\_, ed. *Performing Feminisms: Feminist Critical Theory and Theatre*. Baltimore: Johns Hopkins University Press, 1990.

Chinoy, Helen Krick, and Linda Walsh Jenkins, eds. *Women in American Theatre*. Rev. ed. New York: Theatre Communications Group, 1987.

Chodorow, Nancy. *The Reproduction of Mothering: Psychoanalysis and the Sociology of Gender*. Berkeley: University of California Press, 1978.

Cixous, Helene. "The Laugh of the Medusa." *New French Feminisms: An Anthology*. Eds. Elaine Marks and Isabelle de Courtivron. New York: Schocken Books, 1981. 245–64.

Colaneri, Grace, ed. *Freshman Handbook 1971.* South Hadley, Mass.: Mount Holyoke College, 1971.

Coven, Brenda. *American Women Dramatists of the Twentieth Century: A Bibliography.* Metuchen, N.J.: Scarecrow, 1982.

Cranny-Francis, Anne. *Feminist Fiction.* New York: St. Martin's, 1990.

Curb, Rosemary K. "Re/cognition, Re/presentation, Re/creation in Woman-Conscious Drama: The Seer, the Seen, the Scene, the Obscene." *Theatre Journal* 37 (Oct. 1985): 302–16.

Daly, Mary. *Gyn/Ecology.* Boston: Beacon, 1978.

_____. "Sin Big." *New Yorker* (Special Women's Issue) 26 Feb./4 March 1996: 76+.

Davy, Kate. *Richard Foreman and the Ontological-Hysteric Theatre.* Ann Arbor: UMI Research, 1981.

de Lauretis, Teresa. *Alice Doesn't: Feminism, Semiotics, Cinema.* Bloomington: Indiana University Press, 1984.

_____. *Technologies of Gender: Essays on Theory, Film, and Fiction.* Bloomington: Indiana University Press, 1987.

Denfeld, Rene. "Feminist Movement Has Taken Over by the I-Hate-All-Those-Men Crowd." *Philadelphia Inquirer* 21 April 1995: A27.

_____. *The New Victorians: A Young Woman's Challenge to the Old Feminist Order.* New York: Warner, 1995.

Dolan, Jill. *Presence and Desire: Essays on Gender, Sexuality, Performance.* Ann Arbor: University of Michigan Press, 1993.

_____. *The Feminist Spectator as Critic.* Ann Arbor: University of Michigan Press, 1991.

Dowd, Maureen. "How to Snag 2000 Men." *New York Times* 2 July 1997: A23.

Dubin, Murray. "Mother of a Revolution." *Philadelphia Inquirer* 3 March 1996: H1+.

_____. "Study Denies That Women Are Torn Between Their Career and Family." *Philadelphia Inquirer* 11 May 1995: A3.

Donovan, Josephine. *Feminist Theory: The Intellectual Traditions of American Feminism.* New York: Continuum, 1990.

Ehrenreich, Barbara, and Deidre English. *For Her Own Good: 150 Years of the Experts' Advice to Women.* New York: Doubleday, 1989.

Eisner, Jane. "Can Women Find the Right Balance?" *Philadelphia Inquirer* 3 Sept. 1995: E5.

Elam, Keir. *The Semiotics of Theatre and Drama.* London: Methuen, 1980.

Ellmann, Mary. *Thinking About Women.* New York: Harcourt, 1968.

Faludi, Susan. *Backlash: The Undeclared War Against American Women.* New York: Crown, 1991.

_____. "'I'm Not a Feminist But I Play One on TV.'" *Ms.* 5.5 (March/April 1995): 31–39.

Ferguson, Charles W. *The Male Attitude.* Boston: Little, Brown, 1966.

Fetterley, Judith. *The Resisting Reader: A Feminist Approach to American Fiction.* Bloomington: Indiana University Press, 1978.

French, Marilyn. *The War Against Women*. New York: Ballantine, 1992.
_____. *The Women's Room*. New York: Jove/HBJ, 1977.
Friedan, Betty. *The Feminine Mystique*. New York: Dell, 1974.
_____. *The Second Stage*. New York: Summit Books, 1981.
Galehouse, Maggie. "Camille Paglia Bolsters Her Brawl with Feminism." Review of *Vamps and Tramps: New Essays*, by Camille Paglia. *Philadelphia Inquirer* 4 Dec. 1994: M3.
Gallman, Vanessa. "More Children Living in One-Parent Homes." *Philadelphia Inquirer* 20 July 1994: A3.
Gamman, Lorraine, and Margaret Marshment, eds. *The Female Gaze: Women as Viewers of Popular Culture*. Seattle: Real Comet Press, 1989.
Gettell, President Richard Glenn. "A Plea for the Uncommon Woman." Inaugural Address. MountHolyoke College, 2 Nov. 1957.
Gillespie, Marcia Ann. "A New Day Is Coming." *Ms.* 6.4 (Jan./Feb. 1996): 1.
Gillespie, Patti. "Feminist Theatre: A Rhetorical Phenomenon." *The Quarterly Journal of Speech* 64 (1978): 284–94.
Gledhill, Christine. "Recent Developments in Feminist Criticism." *Quarterly Review of Film Studies* 3 (Fall 1978): 457–93.
Glendon, Mary Ann. "New Feminism Includes All the Women's Issues." *Philadelphia Inquirer* 9 Sept. 1995: A7.
Goodman, Lizbeth. *Contemporary Feminist Theatres: To Each Her Own*. Gender and Performance Series. Eds. Tracy C. Davis and Susan Bassnett. New York: Routledge, 1993.
Grimes, William. "On Stage, and Off." *New York Times* 9 May 1997: Weekend 2.
Handy, Bruce. "Roll Over, Ward Cleaver." *Time* 14 April 1997: 78–85.
Hanisch, Carol. "The Personal Is Political." *Notes from the Second Year: Women's Liberation, Major Writings of the Radical Feminists*. Eds. Shulamith Firestone and Anne Koedt. New York: n.p., 1970. 76–78.
Hart, Lynda, ed. *Making a Spectacle: Feminist Essays on Contemporary Theater*. Ann Arbor: University of Michigan Press, 1989.
Hart, Lynda, and Peggy Phelan. *Acting Out: Feminist Performances*. Ann Arbor: University of Michigan Press, 1993.
Hochman, Gloria. "Are Fathers Obsolete? The New Facts of Life." *Inquirer: The Philadelphia Inquirer Magazine* 17 July 1994: 18+.
Hope, Diane S. "A Rhetorical Definition of Movements: The Drama of Rebirth in Radical Feminism." Unpublished diss., State University of New York at Buffalo, 1975.
Humm, Maggie. *Feminist Criticism: Women as Contemporary Critics*. New York: St. Martin's, 1986.
Irigaray, Luce. "The Sex Which Is Not One." *New French Feminisms: An Anthology*. Eds. Elaine Marks and Isabelle de Courtivron. New York: Schocken, 1981. 99–106.

Jagger, Alison. *Feminist Politics and Human Nature.* Totowa, N.J.: Rowman and Allanheld, 1983.

Jagger, Alison M., and Paula S. Rothenberg, eds. *Feminist Frameworks: Alternative Theoretical Accounts of the Relations Between Women and Men.* 2nd ed. New York: McGraw-Hill, 1984.

Jenkins, Linda. "Locating the Language of Gender Experience." *Women and Performance: A Journal of Feminist Theory* 2 (1984): 5–20.

Jones, Kathleen P. "Citizenship in a Woman-Friendly Polity. "*Signs: Journal of Women in Culture and Society* 15 (1990): 781–812.

Kaminer, Wendy. "Sexual Politics, Continued." Review of *Faces of Feminism: An Activist's Reflection on the Women's Movement,* by Sheila Tobias. *New York Times Book Review* 23 March 1997: 12.

Kaplan, E. Ann. *Women and Film: Both Sides of the Camera.* New York: Methuen, 1983.

Keyssar, Helene. *Feminist Theatre: An Introduction to Plays of Contemporary British and American Women.* New York: Grove, 1985.

Killian, Linda. "Feminist Theatre." *Feminist Art Journal* 3 (1974): 23–24.

Kristeva, Julia. "Woman Can Never Be Defined." *New French Feminisms: An Anthology.* Eds. Elaine Marks and Isabelle de Courtivron. New York: Schocken, 1981. 137–41.

Lane, Eric, and Nina Shengold, eds. *Plays for Actresses.* New York: Vintage, 1997.

Leavitt, Dinah Luise. *Feminist Theatre Groups.* Jefferson, N.C.: McFarland, 1980.

Lerner, Gerda. *The Female Experience.* Indianapolis: Bobbs-Merrill, 1977.

Lorde, Audre. "The Master's Tools Will Never Dismantle the Master's House." *Sister Outsider.* New York: Crossing Press, 1984. 110–13.

MacKinnon, Catherine. "Feminism, Marxism, Method, and the State: An Agenda for Theory." *Modern Feminisms: Political, Literary, Cultural.* Ed. Maggie Humm. New York: Columbia University Press, 1992. 116–21.

Malpede, Karen, ed. *Women in Theater: Compassion and Hope.* 3rd ed. New York: Limelight, 1991.

Margolies-Mezvinsky, Marjorie. "The Female Dilemma." Review of *Beyond the Double Bind: Women and Leadership,* by Kathleen Hall Jamieson. *Philadelphia Inquirer* 7 May 1995: M1.

Marks, Elaine, and Isabelle de Courtivron, eds. *New French Feminisms: An Anthology.* New York: Schocken, 1981.

Marks, Peter. "This Silent Man Has Playwrights as Groupies." *New York Times* 18 Feb. 1996: H5+.

Mayne, Judith. "Feminist Film Theory and Women at the Movies." *Profession 87* (Modern Language Association Annual) 1987: 14–19.

_____. "Review Essay: Feminist Film Theory and Criticism." *Signs* 11 (Autumn 1985): 81–100.

Merrill, Lisa. "Feminist Humor: Rebellious and Self-Affirming." *Women's Studies: An Interdisciplinary Journal* 15,1 (1988): 271–80.

Moi, Toril. *Sexual/Textual Politics*. London: Methuen, 1985.

Morgan, Robin, ed. *Sisterhood Is Powerful: An Anthology of Writings from the Women's Liberation Movement*. New York: Vintage, 1970.

Mulvey, Laura. "Visual Pleasure and Narrative Cinema." *Art after Modernism: Rethinking Representation*. Ed. Brian Wallis. Boston: David R. Godine, 1984. 361–73.

Natalle, Elizabeth J. *Feminist Theater: A Study in Persuasion*. Metuchen, N.J.: Scarecrow, 1985.

Paglia, Camille. *Vamps and Tramps: New Essays*. New York: Vintage, 1994.

Patai, Daphne, and Noretta Koertge. *Professing Feminism*. New York: New Republic, 1994.

Pearson, Carol, and Katherine Pope. *The Female Hero in American and British Literature*. New York: Bowker, 1981.

Pitcher, Harvey. *The Chekhov Play: A New Interpretation*. Berkeley: University of California Press, 1985.

Plotke, David. "Racial Politics and the Clinton-Guinier Episode." *Dissent* 42,2 (Spring 1995): 221–35.

Pollitt, Katha. "Devil Woman." *New Yorker* (Special Women's Issue) 26 Feb./4 March 1996: 58+.

_____. "Forced Sex Is All Too Common." *Philadelphia Inquirer* 4 Dec. 1994: E7.

Povich, Lynn. "Zoë Goes Public." *Working Woman* 19.8 (Aug. 1994): 46–9.

Prasso, Sheri. "Women Still Battle Career Stereotypes, Study Says." *Philadelphia Inquirer* 28 Feb. 1996: C1–2.

Raymond, Janice. "Female Friendship." *Feminist Frameworks: Alternative Theoretical Accounts of the Relations Between Women and Men*. 2nd ed. New York: McGraw-Hill, 1984. 334–39.

Register, Cheri. "American Feminist Literary Criticism: A Bibliographical Introduction." *Feminist Literary Criticism: Explorations in Theory*. Ed. Josephine Donovan. Lexington: University of Kentucky Press, 1975. 1–28.

Reinelt, Janelle. "Feminist Theory and the Problem of Performance." *Modern Drama* 32 (March 1989): 48–57.

Rich, Adrienne. "Compulsory Heterosexuality and Lesbian Existence." *The Signs Reader: Women, Gender, and Scholarship*. Eds. Elizabeth Abel and Emily K. Abel. Chicago: University of Chicago Press, 1983. 139–69.

_____. *Of Woman Born*. New York: Norton, 1976.

_____. "When We Dead Awaken: Writing as Re-Vision." *On Lies, Secrets, and Silence: Selected Prose 1966–1978*. New York: Norton, 1979. 33–49.

Ridley, Clifford A. "Women Are a Force in Area Companies—But to What Extent?" *Philadelphia Inquirer* 25 July 1994: C6.

Roiphe, Katie. *The Morning After: Sex, Fear, and Feminism*. Boston: Little, Brown, 1993.

Rosenfelt, Deborah, and Judith Stacey. "Second Thoughts on the Second Wave." *Feminist Studies* 13 (1987): 341–61.

Russ, Joanna. *How to Suppress Women's Writing.* Austin: University of Texas Press, 1983.

_____. "What's a Heroine to Do? Or, Why Women Can't Write." *Images of Women in Fiction.* Ed. Susan Cornillon. Bowling Green: Bowling Green University Popular Press, 1973. 3–20.

St. George, Donna. "In a Show of Strength, Feminists Gathering." *Philadelphia Inquirer* 2 Feb. 1996: A1, A5.

Saline, Carol. *Sisters.* Photographs by Sharon J. Wohlmuth. Philadelphia: Running Press, 1994.

Sanday, Peggy Reeves. "But the Boys from Cornell Acted Like 2-year-olds." *Philadelphia Inquirer* 27 Nov. 1995: A15.

_____. "Sacrificing Women on the Altar of Centuries-old Stereotypes." *Philadelphia Inquirer* 2 Feb. 1996: A15.

Sarachild, Kathie. "A Program for Feminist 'Consciousness-Raising.'" *Notes from the Second Year: Women's Liberation, Major Writings of the Radical Feminists.* Eds. Shulamith Firestone and Anne Koedt. New York: n.p., 1970. 78–80.

_____. "Consciousness-Raising: A Radical Weapon." *Feminist Revolution.* Ed. Redstockings of the Women's Liberation Movement. New York: Random House, 1975. 144–50.

Schlueter, June, ed. *Feminist Rereadings of Modern American Drama.* Madison, N.J.: Fairleigh Dickinson University Press, 1989.

"Second Attorney General Candidate Withdraws Over Alien Hiring." *Facts on File: World News Digest* 199300236 (11 Feb. 1993): 3pp. Online. Internet. 28 May 1997.

Sexton, Anne. "Housewife." *The Complete Poems.* Boston: Houghton Mifflin, 1981. 77.

Shister, Gail. "TV Talk: Play Day." *Philadelphia Inquirer* 17 April 1997: C8.

Showalter, Elaine. *A Literature of Their Own: British Women Novelists from Brontë to Lessing.* Princeton, N.J.: Princeton University Press, 1977.

_____, ed. *The New Feminist Criticism: Essays on Women, Literature, and Theory.* New York: Pantheon, 1985.

Smiley, Sam. *The Drama of Attack.* Columbia: University of Missouri Press, 1972.

Smith, Anna Deavere. "Broken Sentences." *New Yorker* (Special Women's Issue) 26 Feb./4 March 1996: 158+. Smith, Liz. "Peopletalk." *Philadelphia Inquirer* 29 April 1997: F2.

Sommers, Christina Heff. *Who Stole Feminism? How Women Have Betrayed Women.* New York: Simon and Schuster, 1994.

Steenland, Sally. "Second-guessing Career Women." *Philadelphia Inquirer* 3 April 1997: A15.

Stimpson, Catherine R. *Where the Meanings Are.* New York: Routledge, 1990.

Tanenbaum, Leora. "Anti-Feminist Feminists: The Conservative Attack on Feminism." *Outlook: The Journal of the American Association of University Women* 89,2 (Summer 1995): 8–12.

Tompkins, Jane. *Sensational Designs: The Cultural Work of American Fiction.* New York: Oxford University Press, 1985.

Tong, Rosemarie. *Feminist Thought: A Comprehensive Introduction.* San Francisco: Westview, 1989.

Walker, Alice. *In Search of Our Mothers' Gardens.* New York: Harvest/HBJ, 1983.

Walker, Rebecca, ed. *To Be Real: Telling the Truth and Changing the Face of Feminism.* New York: Anchor, 1995.

Wittig, Monique. "One Is Not Born a Woman." *Feminist Issues* 1(Winter 1981): 47–54.

Wolf, Naomi. *Fire with Fire: The New Female Power and How It Will Change the 21st Century.* New York: Random House,1993.

_____. "Pro-Choice *and* Pro-Life." *New York Times* 3 April 1997: A21.

Woolf, Virginia. *A Room of One's Own.* New York: Harcourt, 1929.

Young, Cathy. "And Let's Have Balance at Beijing Women's Conference." *Philadelphia Inquirer* 3 Sept. 1995: E5.

_____. "Fresh Perspective on the Gender Wars in a Book of Essays." Review of *Reasonable Creatures: Essays on Women and Feminism,* by Katha Pollitt. *Philadelphia Inquirer* 4 Dec. 1994: M3.

_____. "Gender Internet Wars Aren't Just One-sided." *Philadelphia Inquirer* 27 Nov. 1995: A15.

_____. "Iron Men and Ironies Confront Feminists." *Philadelphia Inquirer* 28 Jan. 1996: E9.

_____. "Radical Feminists Invoke Old Image of Female Frailty." *Philadelphia Inquirer* 4 Dec. 1994: E7.

_____. Review of *Promiscuities: The Secret Struggle for Womanhood,* by Naomi Wolf. *Philadelphia Inquirer* 13 July 1997: Q3.

Zeidner, Lisa. "Lawyer Gives Women Straight Talk about Negotiating at Home." Review of *Kidding Ourselves: Breadwinning, Babies, and Bargaining Power,* by Rhona Mahony. *Philadelphia Inquirer* 2 July 1995: F3.

# Index

Albright, Patricia 35, 61, 155
Allen, Joan 59, 70, 72
Allen, Woody 134
*An American Daughter* 4, 5, 13, 14, 15, 19–20, 22, 24, 100–126, 128, 133, 134–137, 140, 141, 146, 147, 154–155
antifeminist 5, 8, 118
*Antonia and Jane* 146
*Any Woman Can't* 128
Aristotle 129
Austin, Gayle 10, 12, 150, 157

*Bachelor Girls* 5, 24, 27, 28, 42, 43–44, 49, 53, 59, 61, 64, 72, 116–117, 143
Baird, Zoë 101, 109, 111
Barnes, Clive 49, 64, 82, 84, 85, 87, 93, 110, 112, 118, 125, 134, 150, 152, 154
Barney, Lee 33, 56, 78, 82, 86, 89, 91, 93, 94, 133, 155
Beaufort, John 31, 32, 75, 149, 150
Betsko, Kathleen 1, 21, 25, 26, 33, 34, 37, 39, 42, 45, 49, 53, 130, 145
Bishop, Andre 115
Black, Kent 42, 155
Bogart, Paul 140, 147
Brantley, Ben 106, 115, 119, 122, 123, 124
Breyer, Stephen 109
Brown, Helen Gurley 78
Brown, Janet 11–12, 157
Brustein, Robert 18, 63, 64, 76, 91, 98, 151, 152, 154
Burleigh, Nina 56, 70, 76, 78, 82, 137, 155

Carlson, Susan 19, 32, 37, 149
Carter, Bill 128, 155
Case, Sue-Ellen 13, 16–17, 39, 47, 157
Chekhov, Anton 82, 134
Chodorow, Nancy 44, 157
Christy, Marian 76, 155
circular writing *see* cyclic writing
Cixous, Helene 16, 158
Clinton, Bill 101
Clinton, Hillary Rodham 101, 112, 113, 116
Cohen, Esther 10, 14, 16, 21, 22, 27, 33, 42, 146
Coleman, Cy 127
consciousness-raising 11, 14, 57, 59, 60, 61, 62–63, 64, 66, 67, 68, 69, 74, 133
Corliss, Richard 42, 48, 150
Cuervo, Alma 33–34, 147
Curb, Rosemary 10–11, 14, 158
cyclic writing 1, 14, 16–17, 18, 19, 40, 84, 102, 132, 133

Daly, Mary 1–2, 158
Denfeld, Rene 7, 8, 158
Dickinson, Emily 21, 35
Dolan, Jill 3–6, 12, 14, 17, 23, 53–54, 63, 129, 130, 158
Dowd, Maureen 118, 158
Durang, Christopher 128

Eder, Richard 23, 29–30, 34, 134, 149
Eisner, Jane 50, 158
"either/or" 6, 25, 46, 47, 63, 78, 97, 100, 102, 104, 133
Elder, Sharon 35, 76, 77, 78, 136, 155

Evans, Greg 101, 104, 106, 109, 115, 120, 134, 154

Faludi, Susan 8, 9, 88, 158
Feingold, Michael 87, 88–89, 122, 123, 152, 154
fem-en(act)ment 1–2, 10, 12, 17–18, 20, 56, 84, 127, 131–132, 135, 137
"feminine mystique" 41, 43, 44, 48, 49, 50, 78, 136
feminism 1, 2–11, 14, 20, 23, 25, 31, 34, 37, 38, 41, 47, 50, 52, 54, 56, 57, 58, 59–60, 62, 63, 65, 66, 68, 69, 71, 73, 75–76, 78, 80, 82, 83, 84, 85, 86, 89, 96, 100, 101, 107, 114, 115, 116, 117–121, 124, 125, 126, 128, 130–133, 135–137
feminist drama 4, 9, 10, 11, 12, 14, 18, 39
"feminist mystique" 6, 28, 48
feminist theatre 10, 11, 13
Finn, William 10, 55, 91, 99, 155
Franklin, Nancy 101, 105, 111, 112, 113, 115, 118, 119–120, 122, 123–124, 134, 135, 149, 155
French, Marilyn 9, 159
Friedan, Betty 6, 28, 41, 48, 78, 159

Gates, Anita 34, 39, 149
Gerard, Jeremy 63, 65, 72, 93, 151, 152
Gettell, Richard Glenn 29, 159
Gillespie, Patti 11, 159
The Girl from Fargo: A Play 143
Glendon, Mary Ann 136–137, 159
Gold, Sylviane 62, 64, 66, 69, 70, 77–78, 79, 151
Greene, Alexis 85, 94, 99, 152
Greer, Germaine 27
Grimes, William 122, 159
Grossberg, Michael 86, 155
Gussow, Mel 41, 43, 44, 50, 54, 58, 61, 63, 64, 70, 78, 85, 92, 96, 99, 150, 151, 153
Gutierrez, Gerald 140
gynomorphic language 2

Happy Birthday, Montpelier Pa-zazz 128, 146
Harris, Mark 122, 154
Hart, Lynda 3, 75, 159
"having it all" 6, 19, 20, 23, 49–51, 52, 54, 57, 70, 78, 96, 100, 101–102, 104, 107, 109, 117, 119, 120, 121, 125, 129, 132
Hawthorne, Nathaniel 129
Heffley, Lynne 131, 155
The Heidi Chronicles 1, 3, 4, 5, 9, 10–11, 12, 14, 15, 18, 19, 22, 27, 37, 46, 52, 56–80, 81, 84, 87, 104, 116, 133, 135, 140, 141, 143, 146, 147, 150–152
Hemingway, Ernest 137
Henry, William A. 86, 92, 151, 153
Hoban, Phoebe 85, 90, 92, 95, 99, 134, 155
Hodgins, Paul 81–82, 89, 98, 153
Hodgson, Moira 57, 151
Holbrook, Hal 125, 147
How to Marry a Millionaire Part Two, or She Did So Well 146
Hubbard, Kim 24, 25, 31, 56, 78, 156

Isn't It Romantic 4, 5, 8, 12, 14, 16, 19, 22, 24, 40–55, 63, 68, 70, 78, 84, 89, 97, 101, 135, 139–140, 143, 150

Jackness, Andrew 143
Jagger, Alison 63, 160
Jewish themes 45, 82–84, 85, 91, 94, 95, 99, 103, 122
Jill's Adventure in Real Estate or, I Can Get It for You at 3.2 143
Jones, Kathleen P. 73, 160

Kahn, Madeline 95, 147
Kakutani, Michiko 40, 47, 49, 54, 150
Kalem, T.E. 1, 36, 37, 149
Kaminer, Wendy 117, 118, 160
Kennedy, Dana 133, 151
Kent, Arthur 110
Keyssar, Helene 73, 151, 160
Kirkpatrick, Melanie 84, 98, 153
Kissel, Howard 58, 63, 77, 83–84, 86, 93, 151, 153

Kozikowski, Thomas 22, 23, 32, 34, 35, 37, 134, 156
Kraft, Daphne 86, 95, 153
Kramer, Mimi 57, 64, 75, 151
Kroll, Jack 89, 92, 95, 151, 153
Kron, Joan 94, 153

Leavitt, Dinah 3, 10, 11, 14, 15, 26, 160
"l'écriture feminine" 16
Leonard, John 72, 78, 151
Levis, Georgette (Wasserstein) 15, 94, 156
Lipson, Karen 61, 151
Lorde, Audre 13, 160
Lurie, Alison 81
Lynch, Thomas 61
lyric mode 17, 123, 124, 125

MacKinnon, Catherine 7, 160
*Maids in America* 146
"male gaze" 10
*The Man in a Case* 128, 143
Mandl, Bette 66, 68, 73, 77, 79, 131, 151
Marks, Peter 100–101, 107, 115, 116, 117, 119, 125, 154, 160
Matuz, Roger 77, 156
McCauley, Stephen 127
McGuigan, Cathleen 15, 30, 57, 68, 70, 76, 151
McNally, Terrence 143, 147
Mehta, Sonny 128
Merrill, Lisa 16, 161
Meyer, Sandra (Wasserstein) 15, 50, 89–90, 91, 94, 99
*Miami* 84, 128, 146
Millennium Project 128
Miller, Judith 43, 81, 84, 90, 93, 94, 127, 156
Millet, Kate 27
Moi, Toril 4, 161
Moore, Mary Tyler 134
Morgan, Robin 15, 161
Moritz, Charles 41, 57, 156
Mossman, Merrily 139, 147
mother-daughter paradigm 4, 5, 19, 42–44, 50–51, 53–54, 79, 91–92, 99, 114, 132, 133

Mulvey, Laura 10, 161
*Mutz* 146

Nannygate 101, 109, 111, 117, 120
Natalle, Elizabeth 11, 13, 14, 15, 24, 34, 161
neofeminism 101, 103, 118, 120, 121
Newton, Edmund 30, 32, 36, 149
Nightingale, Benedict 44–45, 47, 48, 50, 53, 150

*The Object of My Affection* 127
O'Connor, John 64, 151
O'Connor, John J. 34, 149
O'Keeffe, Georgia 61, 80
*Old Money* (tentative title) 135
Oliver, Edith 94, 150, 153, 156

Paglia, Camille 88, 161
*Pamela's First Musical* 127, 131, 143
Parker, Ellen 39, 147
Parks, Steve 125, 150
Phelan, Peggy 3, 75, 159
Pitcher, Harvey 134, 161
"playful pluralism" 3, 4
Povich, Lynn 109, 161
Prasso, Sheri 98, 161
Pulitzer Prize 1, 56, 81

*The Queen of Mababahwe* 147

Richards, David 61, 64, 68, 79, 82, 85, 86, 90, 92, 93, 94, 95, 151, 153
Ridley, Clifford 122, 125, 154, 161
Robins, Corinne 75, 77, 151
Robman, Stephen 139, 140, 147
Roiphe, Katie 7, 161
Rose, Lloyd 104, 106, 110, 112, 116, 118, 124, 154
Rosenfelt, Deborah 76, 162
Rothman, Carole 139, 147
Rothstein, Mervyn 58, 59, 61, 62, 70, 71, 72, 73, 151
Russ, Joanna 17, 123, 162

Saline, Carol 94, 99, 162
Schwartz, Felice 97–98
Sexton, Anne 40, 162
sexual politics 109, 115–116, 120
Shapiro, Walter 15, 58, 71, 72, 80, 89, 109, 111, 118, 120, 122, 125, 151, 154
Sheward, David 101, 111, 122, 154
Simon, John 35, 43, 48, 61, 63, 67, 69, 78, 92, 93–94, 95, 149, 150, 151, 153
Simon, Neil 134
sisterhood 19, 37, 52, 56, 63, 64, 65, 66–69, 70, 72, 73–74, 77, 98, 116, 117, 118, 120, 132, 133, 136
*The Sisters Rosensweig* 4, 5, 13, 14, 15, 19, 20, 21–22, 81–99, 100, 102, 103, 107, 123, 128, 132, 133, 134, 135, 140, 141, 143, 147, 152–154
*Smart Women, Brilliant Choices (Urban Blight* segment) 128, 146
Sommers, Christina Hoff 7–8, 162
Span, Paula 76, 78, 137, 151
Specter, Michael 95, 153
Speers, W. 122, 154
Spencer, David 120, 124, 125, 154
Stacey, Judith 76, 162
Stearns, David Patrick 56, 71, 75, 86–87, 95, 109, 113, 114, 115, 120, 151, 153, 154
Stein, Howard 16, 25, 26, 39, 85, 86, 92, 134, 156
Stone, Lu 84–85, 146
Stuart, Jan 82, 83, 85, 86, 89, 94, 96, 99, 153
Sullivan, Andrew 109, 128
Sullivan, Dan 61, 99, 140, 147
"superwoman" 69, 70, 71, 49–50, 57, 67

Tanenbaum, Leora 8, 9, 163
*Tender Offer* 128, 143
Thigpen, Lynne 122, 147
Tompkins, Jane 129, 131, 163
Tong, Rosemarie 89, 163
Tony Awards 59, 95, 122

*Uncommon Women and Others* 1, 5, 10–11, 12, 13–14, 15, 18–19, 21, 22, 23, 24, 25, 26, 27–39, 40, 41, 52, 54, 67, 86, 97, 135, 139, 141, 143, 147, 149–150

Vellela, Tony 95, 153

Wasserstein, Lola 42, 43, 44, 91
Wasserstein, Morris 94
Wasserstein, Wendy: archival material 67, 77; articles by 2, 9, 33, 49, 50, 67, 90, 137, 144–145; personal interview with 50, 51, 57, 58, 62, 68, 77, 78, 84, 96, 97, 121, 123, 127, 128, 132, 135, 146; speeches by 14, 33, 42, 58, 61, 82, 98, 145; telephone interview with 107, 110, 127, 128, 135, 136, 146; *see also* specific works
Watt, Douglas 29, 33, 35, 82–83, 91, 92, 134, 150, 151, 153
Weales, Gerald 67, 71, 78, 151
*When Dinah Shore Ruled the World* 128
Williams, Jeannie 109, 111, 125, 155
Winer, Laurie 72, 73, 74, 75, 151
Winer, Linda 57, 67, 70, 76, 83, 87, 88, 90, 94, 102, 106, 111, 114, 115, 125–126, 151, 154, 155
Wolf, Naomi 3, 7, 118, 163
"woman-conscious drama" 10, 11, 12, 14
women's movement 1, 7, 18, 21, 22, 25, 27, 30, 39, 40, 49, 56, 57, 66, 68, 69, 75–78, 79–80, 81, 86, 107, 115, 117, 121, 132, 136, 137
Wood, Dana 111, 131, 156
Wood, Kimba 101, 109, 111
*Workout* 128–129, 143

Young, Cathy 4, 118, 163